C++ FOR C PROGRAMMERS

Other Titles of Interest

C++ for C Programmers

Ira Pohl

University of California, Santa Cruz

The Benjamin/Cummings Publishing Company, Inc.

Redwood City, California ■ Fort Collins, Colorado
Menlo Park, California ■ Reading, Massachusetts ■ New York
Don Mills, Ontario ■ Wokingham, U.K. ■ Amsterdam ■ Bonn
Sydney ■ Singapore ■ Tokyo ■ Madrid ■ San Juan

Sponsoring Editor: Alan Apt
Associate Editor: Mark McCormick
Production Coordinator: Linda Seals,
    B. Vader Design/Production
Text and Cover Design: Linda Seals,
    B. Vader Design/Production
Copy Editor: Carol Dondrea
Composition: Graphic Typesetting Service

LIBRARY OF CONGRESS CATALOGING-IN-PUBLICATION DATA

Pohl, Ira.
    C++ for C programmers / Ira Pohl.
        p.   cm.
    Includes index.
    ISBN 0-8053-0910-1
    1. C++ (Computer program language)   I. Title.
QA76.73.C153P64   1989
005.13′3−dc19   89-117
                                                                             CIP

ISBN 0-8053-0910-1

5 6 7 8 9 10 AL 95949392

The Benjamin/Cummings Publishing Company, Inc.
390 Bridge Parkway
Redwood City, California 94065

PREFACE

This book is intended as a gentle introduction to programming in C++ for the programmer or student already familiar with C. Its approach is to use an evolutionary teaching process with C as a starting point. The programmer can stop and use the language facilities up to that point in the text. We start with C and end with C++. The book is a tutorial on C++ programming.

C++ is a powerful modern successor language to C. It was invented at Bell Labs by Bjarne Stroustrup in the mid-1980s. C++ adds to C the concept of *class*, a mechanism for providing user-defined types also called *abstract data types*. It supports *object-oriented* programming by these means and by providing inheritance and run-time type binding. C is the present; C++ is the future.

By carefully developing working C++ programs, using the method of *dissection*, this book presents a simple and thorough introduction to the programming process in C++. Dissection is a technique for explaining new elements in a program that the student is seeing for the first time. It highlights key points in the many examples of working code that is used to teach by example.

This book is intended for use in a first course in programming in C++. It can be used as a supplementary text in an advanced programming course, data structures course, software methodology course, comparative language course, or other courses where the instructor wants C++ to be the language of choice. Each chapter presents a number of carefully explained programs. Many programs and functions are dissected.

All the major pieces of code were tested. A consistent and proper coding style is adopted from the beginning. The style standard used is one chosen by professionals in the C community.

For the programmer who has no C experience, this book should be used in conjunction with *A Book on C* by Al Kelley and Ira Pohl (Benjamin/Cummings, Menlo Park, Calif., 1984). As a package, the two books offer an integrated treatment of the C and C++ programming languages and their use that is unavailable elsewhere.

Each chapter has:

Dissections. A program particularly illustrative of the themes of that chapter is analyzed by dissection. Dissection is similar to a structured walk-through of the code. Its intention is to explain to the reader newly encountered programming elements and idioms.

Summary. A succinct list of points covered in the chapter are reiterated as helpful review.

Exercises. The exercises test the student's knowledge of the language. Many exercises are intended to be done interactively while reading the text. This encourages self-paced instruction by the reader. The exercises also frequently extend the reader's knowledge to an advanced area of use.

The book incorporates:

An Evolutionary Approach. The C programmer can immediately benefit from programming in C++. The early chapters show how the language is improved by stronger typing, a new comment style, call-by-reference, and other useful minor additions. Many of these changes are similar to ones in the new ANSI standard C. The middle chapters show how classes work. Classes are the basis for abstract data types and object-oriented programming. Again the student starts from the C perspective and moves to the C++ view. The later chapters give advanced details of the use of inheritance and stream I/O. At any point in the text the programmer can stop and use the new material.

Teaching by Example. The book is a tutorial that stresses examples of working code. Right from the start the student is introduced to full working programs. An interactive environment is assumed. Exercises are integrated with the examples to encourage experimentation. Excessive detail is avoided in explaining the larger elements of writing working code. Each chapter has several important example programs. Major elements of these programs are explained by the method of dissection.

Data Structures in C++. The text emphasizes many of the standard data structures from computer science. Stacks, safe arrays, dynamically allocated multidimensional arrays, lists, trees, and strings are all implemented. Exercises extend the student's understanding of how to implement and use these structures. Implementation is consistent with an abstract data type approach to software.

Object-Oriented Programming. The reader is led gradually to the object-oriented style. Chapter 0 and Chapter 1 discuss how the C programmer can benefit in important ways from a switch to C++ and object-oriented programming. The terminology of object-oriented concepts are defined and the way in which these concepts are supported by C++ is introduced. Chapter 3 introduces classes. This is the basic mechanism for producing modular programs and implementing abstract data types. Class variables are the *objects* being manipulated. Chapter 6 develops inheritance and virtual functions, two key elements in this paradigm. Chapter 8 integrates all the previous techniques showing how to properly write multicomponent programs in an object-oriented style.

Acknowledgments

My special thanks go to my wife, Debra Dolsberry, who encouraged me throughout this project. She acted as technical editor and implemented and tested all major pieces of code. Her careful implementations of the code and exercises often led to important improvements. Others who provided helpful suggestions include: Skona Brittain; Al Conrad; Steve Demurjian; Samuel Druker, Zortech Limited; Robert Durling; Bruce Eckel; Daniel Edelson; Gene Fisher; Robert Hansen, Lattice, Incorporated; Kevin Karplus; Al Kelley; Jim Kempf, Sun Microsystems, Incorporated; Ellen Mickanin; and Linda Werner. In addition, my editors Alan Apt and Mark McCormick were very supportive. Finally, I thank Bjarne Stroustrup for inventing such an elegant language and encouraging others to help develop and teach it.

Ira Pohl
University of California, Santa Cruz

To Laura and her mother

CONTENTS

CHAPTER 0

From C to Object-Oriented Programming in C++

C is the natural starting point for C++ because many key ideas in C++ are extensions of C. C++ was created by Bjarne Stroustrup in the early 1980s. Stroustrup had two main goals: (1) C++ was to be compatible with ordinary C, and (2) it was to extend C using the class construct of Simula 67. The class construct is an extension of the C struct. The language, in an early form, is described in B. Stroustrup, *The C++ Programming Language* [1]. Important additions to the current language are described in B. Stroustrup, *The Evolution of C++: 1985 to 1987* [2].

This book teaches C++ to programmers already familiar with C [3]. It does this by building from C to C++. Two aspects of C++ as a successor language to C are stressed. The first is C++'s superiority to C as a general-purpose programming language because of its new features. The second is the success of C++ as an *object-oriented* programming language. In the next section we define what this new concept means.

1

A major premise of our approach is that C++ is a superior C even not taking into consideration the extensions to classes. We expect that C++ will replace C as a general-purpose programming language. With C++ the C programmer can improve on ordinary C code in a number of ways that will be illustrated in Chapters 1 and 2.

0.1. Object-Oriented Programming

We will be using the terms *abstract data type (ADT)* and *object-oriented programming (OOP)* to refer to a powerful new programming approach. An ADT is a user-defined extension to the existing types available in the language. It consists of a set of values and a collection of operations that can act on those values. For example, C does not have a complex number type, but C++ provides the class construct to add such a type and integrate it with existing types. *Objects* are class variables. Object-oriented programming allows ADTs to be easily created and used. OOP uses the mechanism of *inheritance* to conveniently derive a new type from an existing user-defined type. It allows the programmer to model the objects found in the problem domain by programming their content and behavior with a class.

The new class construct in C++ provides the *encapsulation* mechanism to implement ADTs. Encapsulation packages both the internal implementation details of the type and the externally available operations and functions that can act on objects of that type. The implementation details can be made inaccessible to client code that uses the type. For example, stack might be implemented as a fixed-length array, while the publicly available operations would include push and pop. Changing the internal implementation to a linked list should not affect how push and pop are used externally. The implementation of stack is hidden from its clients. The details of how to provide data hiding in classes are touched on in Chapter 1 and developed thoroughly in Chapters 3 and 6.

0.2. Why C++ Is a Better C

Since C++ is based on C, it retains much of that language, including: a rich operator set, nearly orthogonal design, terseness, and extensibility. C++ is a highly portable language, and translators for it exist on many different machines and systems. C++ compilers are highly compatible with existing C programs because maintaining such compatibility was a design objective. Unlike other object-oriented languages, such as Smalltalk, C++ is an extension of an existing language in wide use on many machines.

If C++ is viewed as an object-oriented language alternative to Smalltalk, it is a relatively inexpensive alternative. Programming in C++ does not require a graphics environment, nor do C++ programs incur run-time expense from type checking or garbage collection.

C++ improves on C in significant ways, especially in supporting strong typing. The function prototype syntax, as now required by ANSI C [4][5], is a C++ innovation. In general, C++ has stronger type rules than C, which makes it a safer language.

C++ is a marriage of the low level with the high level. As Stroustrup states [1], "C is at the machine level, while C++ is at the problem domain level." The user can write code at the level appropriate to the problem, while still maintaining contact with the machine-level implementation details.

Operators can be given new definitions based on the types of their arguments. This operator overloading supports the implementation of new types that may be operated upon transparently. Normal functions, like operators, may be overloaded.

There is less reliance on the preprocessor. C programs often use the preprocessor to implement constants and useful macros. However, parameterized #define macros introduce insecurities. In C++, the inline keyword requests the compiler to compile a function as a macro. This preserves type checking while increasing run-time performance compared to normal functions. Reliance on the preprocessor is further diminished by the const type modifier, which specifies that an object is read-only.

There are a large number of other improvements. A favorite of programmers is the addition of the // symbol for one-line comments. There is also a convenient new I/O library. The *stream.h* library provides a very useful alternative to *stdio.h*. The new and delete operators provide convenient access to free store.

Abstract data types are implemented in C++ through the class mechanism. Classes allow a programmer to control the visibility of the underlying implementation. What is public is accessible and what is private is hidden. Data hiding is one component of object-oriented programming. Classes have member functions, including those that overload operators. Member functions allow the programmer to code the appropriate functionality for the ADT. Classes can be defined through an inheritance mechanism that allows for improved code sharing and library development. Inheritance is another hallmark of object-oriented programming.

C is often criticized as a weakly typed unsafe language [6]. However, C++ is strongly typed. Conversions between types are allowed, provided they are well defined. In fact, the language allows the programmer to create conversion functions between arbitrary types.

Parameter passing in C is unchecked with regard to type or number of actual parameters. This leads to bugs that the compiler cannot catch. In C++, function prototypes allow functions to be fully checked as to count and type. Functions taking variable types or numbers of arguments are also supported. The addition of function prototypes is an aid to the programmer, bringing into the compiler checking that was previously obtainable only through *lint*.

The C array model is pointer-based and one-dimensional without bounds checking. This lack of multidimensional arrays means the programmer must spend more time and effort implementing them using the one-dimensional storage mapping function that is C's paradigm. Development and use of dynamic arrays also requires significant work and is not supported in the language. C++ retains the array handling of C; however, classes provide a satisfactory means of transparently implementing general arrays. Multidimensional, dynamic, and bounds-checked arrays can be implemented in libraries.

By and large, the semantics of C++ are much more stringently defined than those of C. For example, type conversion and typing are more carefully implemented. The C need for preprocessor extensibility is curtailed: Function overloading and `inline` can be used to replace macros with arguments, and the `const` type modifier is sufficient for most named constants. The preprocessor's primary remaining uses are file inclusion and conditional compilation.

0.3. Why Switch to C++?

C++ supports the object-oriented programming style. A chief cost is the increased complexity of the language. (Given C++'s objectives this is hardly surprising.) Although the benefits gained by living within the C family and adding improved interface schemes outweigh this cost, the complexity that C++ adds to the C language is one of its biggest drawbacks. C++ has 42 keywords, an increase of 45 percent over traditional C's 29. This increase reflects the large number of needed new ideas, but makes mastery more difficult. To overcome this problem, this book approaches the learning process by gradually transforming the C programmer into a practiced C++ programmer. Each chapter extends from the previous chapter the range of ideas the programmer may use. At any point, the reader can stop and still be partly proficient in C++. In effect, the reader evolves from a standard C programmer to an object-oriented C++ programmer.

C++ is the language of the future. It is supported by AT&T, and several major computer firms, as well as many universities, are committed to its increased use.

C++ is a better C. There is increased convenience in writing code and increased security in the code. Features such as `//` for single-line comments, `const` and `inline`, `new` and `delete` for storage management, and call-by-reference parameters simplify the coding process over C. Stronger typing in general, and function prototypes in particular, enhance security and facilitate software methodology.

0.4. References

1. B. Stroustrup, *The C++ Programming Language*, Addison-Wesley, Reading, Mass., 1986.
   The de facto language reference manual. This book is very difficult reading.
2. B. Stroustrup, *The Evolution of C++: 1985 to 1987*, appears in 1987 USENIX C++ Papers, Santa Fe, N.M., 1987, pp. 1–21.
   Brings his book up-to-date with version 2 language changes.
3. A. Kelley and I. Pohl, *A Book on C*, Benjamin/Cummings, Menlo Park, Calif., 1984.
   A comprehensive text on the C programming language. It is written in the style of this book.
4. A. Kelley and I. Pohl, *Turbo C*, Benjamin/Cummings, Menlo Park, Calif., 1988.
   A tutorial introduction to a popular ANSI C compiler.
5. S. P. Harbison and G. L. Steele, *C: A Reference Manual*, 2d ed., Prentice-Hall, Englewood Cliffs, N.J., 1987.
   The authoritative reference book on the syntax and semantics of the C programming language.
6. I. Pohl and D. Edelson, *A-Z: C Language Shortcomings*, in *Computer Languages*, vol. 13, no. 2, 1988, pp. 51–64.
   A brief paper criticizing 26 defects in the original C language.

CHAPTER 1

An Overview of C++ and Object-Oriented Programming

This chapter gives an overview of the C++ programming language. It also provides an introduction to C++'s use as an object-oriented programming language. Like the rest of the book, it assumes a knowledge of the C programming language. In the chapter a series of programs is presented, and the elements of each program are carefully explained. The programs increase in complexity, and the examples in the later sections illustrate some of the concepts of object-oriented programming. This approach should give the student a sense of how the language works.

Each feature of C++ is explained briefly. Later chapters will explain each new concept in detail. The examples in this chapter give simple, immediate hands-on experience with key features of the C++ language. The chapter introduces the reader to stream I/O, operator and function overloading, reference parameters, classes, constructors, destructors, and inheritance. The system used is the CC translator developed by Bjarne Stroustrup, running under UNIX.

Object-oriented programming is implemented in the class construct. The `class` construct in C++ is an extension of `struct` in C. The later examples in this chapter illustrate how C++ implements OOP concepts, such as data hiding, ADTs, inheritance and type hierarchies.

1.1. Output

Programs must communicate to be useful. Our first example is a program that prints on the screen the phrase "C++ is an improved C.". The complete program is

```
//A first C++ program illustrating output.

#include <stream.h>

main()
{
    cout << "C++ is an improved C.\n";
}
```

The program prints on the screen

```
C++ is an improved C.
```

▓ DISSECTION OF THE *advert* PROGRAM

```
//A first C++ program illustrating output.
```

- The double slash `//` is a new comment symbol. The comment runs to the end of the line. The old C bracketing comment symbols `/* */` are still available for multiline comments.

```
#include <stream.h>
```

- The *stream.h* header introduces I/O facilities for C++.

```
cout << "C++ is an improved C.\n";
```

- This statement prints to the screen. The identifier cout is
  the name of the standard output stream. The operator <<
  passes the string "C++ is an improved C. \n" to standard
  out. Used in this way the << is referred to as the *put to* or
  insertion operator.

We can rewrite our first program as follows.

```
//A first C++ program illustrating output.

#include <stream.h>

main()
{
    cout << "C++ is an improved C." << "\n";
}
```

Although it is different from the first version, it produces the same
output. Each time the << is used with cout, printing continues from the
position where it previously left off. In this case the newline character
is output after a second use of the put to operator.

1.2. Input

We will write a program to convert to kilometers the distance in miles
from the earth to the moon. In miles this distance is, on average, 238,857
miles. This number is an integer. To convert miles to kilometers, we
multiply by the conversion factor 1.609, a real number.

Our conversion program will use variables capable of storing integer values and real values. In C++ all variables must be declared before
their use, but unlike in C, they need not be at the head of a block.
Declarations may be mixed in with executable statements. Their scope,

however, is still the block within which they are declared. Identifiers
should be chosen to reflect their use in the program. In this way, they
serve as documentation, making the program more readable.

```
//The distance to the moon converted to kilometers.

#include <stream.h>

main()
{
    const int moon = 238857;
    cout << "The moon's distance from Earth is " << moon;
    cout << " miles.\n";

    int moon_kilo;
    moon_kilo = moon * 1.609;
    cout << "In kilometers this is " << moon_kilo;
    cout << " km.\n";
}
```

The output of the program is

```
The moon's distance from Earth is 238857 miles.
In kilometers this is 384320 km.
```

■ DISSECTION OF THE *moon* PROGRAM

```
const int moon = 238857;
```

- The keyword const is new in C++. It replaces some uses
  of the preprocessor command define to create named lit-
  erals. Using this type modifier informs the compiler that
  the initialized value of moon cannot be changed.

```
cout << "The moon's distance from Earth is " << moon;
```

- The stream I/O in C++ can discriminate among a variety
  of simple values without needing additional formatting

information. Here the value of moon will be printed as an integer.

```
int moon_kilo;
moon_kilo = moon * 1.609;
```

- Declarations can occur after executable statements. This allows declarations of variables to be nearer to their use.

Let us write a program that will convert a series of values from miles to kilometers. The program will be interactive. The user will type in a value in miles and the program will convert this value to kilometers and print it out.

```
//Miles are converted to kilometers.

#include <stream.h>
const float m_to_k = 1.609;
inline int convert(int mi) { return (mi * m_to_k); }

main()
{
    int miles;

    do {
        cout << "Input distance in miles: ";
        cin >> miles;
        cout << "\nDistance is " << convert(miles) << " km.\n";
    } while (miles > 0);
}
```

This program uses the input stream variable cin, which is normally standard input. The *input operator* >> is called the *get from* or *extraction* operator, that assigns values from the input stream to a variable. This program illustrates both input and output.

■ DISSECTION OF THE *mi_km* PROGRAM

```
const float m_to_k = 1.609;
inline int convert(int mi) { return (mi * m_to_k); }
```

- C++ reduces C's traditional reliance on the preprocessor. For example, instead of having to use `define`, special constants, such as the conversion factor 1.609, are simply assigned to variables specified as constants. The new keyword `inline` specifies that a function is to be compiled, if possible as a macro. As a rule, `inline` should be done sparingly and only on short functions. Also note how the parameter `mi` is declared within the function parentheses. C++ uses *function prototypes* to define and declare functions. This will be explained in the next section.

```
do {
    cout << "Input distance in miles: ";
    cin >> miles;
    cout << "\nDistance is " << convert(miles) << " km. \n";
} while (miles > 0);
```

- The program repeatedly prompts the user for a distance in miles. The program is terminated by a zero or negative value. The value placed in the standard input stream is automatically converted to an integer value assigned to `miles`.

1.3. Function Prototypes

The syntax of functions in C++ inspired the new function prototype syntax found in ANSI C compilers. Basically, the types of parameters are listed inside the header parentheses. By explicitly listing the type and number of arguments, strong type checking and assignment-compatible conversions are possible in C++. The following example illustrates these points:

```
//A program illustrating function prototypes.

#include <stream.h>

main()
{
    int     add3(int, int, int);
    float   average(int);
    int     score_1, score_2, score_3, sum;

    cout << "\nEnter 3 scores: ";
    cin >> score_1 >> score_2 >> score_3;
    sum = add3(score_1, score_2, score_3);
    cout << "\nTheir sum is " << sum << ".\n";
    cout << "\nTheir average is " << average(sum) << ".\n";
    sum = add3(1.5 * score_1, score_2, score_3);
    cout << "\nThe weighted sum is " << sum << ".\n";
    cout << "\nTheir average is " << average(sum) << ".\n";
}

int add3(int a, int b, int c)
{
    return (a + b + c);
}

float average (int s)
{
    return (s / 3.0);
}
```

■ DISSECTION OF THE *add3* PROGRAM

```
int     add3(int, int, int);
float average(int);
```

● These declarations at the head of main are function prototypes. They inform the compiler of the type and number
   of arguments to expect for each externally specified function. The list of arguments can optionally include variable
   names. So,

```
int add3(int a, int b, int c);
```

is also possible.

```
sum = add3(1.5 * score_1, score_2, score_3);
```

- This would not be correct in traditional C. In traditional C, the first argument `1.5 * score_1` is promoted to `double` and passed unconverted to a local place holder expecting an integer. In C++ this expression is converted to an integer value as per the function prototype specification. This single change markedly improves C++ program reliability over traditional C.

```
int add3(int a, int b, int c)
{
    return (a + b + c);
}
```

- Here is the actual function definition. It could just as well have been imported from another file. It is compatible with the function prototype declaration in `main`.

1.4. Classes and Abstract Data Types

What is truly novel about C++ is its aggregate type `class`, which the language introduces. A `class` is an extension of the idea of `struct` in traditional C. A `class` provides the means for implementing a user-defined data type and associated functions and operators. Therefore a `class` is an implementation of an abstract data type. Let us write a `class` called `string` that will implement a restricted form of string.

```
//An elementary implementation of type string.

#include <string.h>
#include <stream.h>

const int max_len = 255;

class string {
   char s[max_len];
   int  len;
public:
   void assign(char* st) { strcpy(s, st); len = strlen(st); }
   int  length() { return (len); }
   void print() { cout << s << "\nLength: " << len << "\n"; }
};
```

Two important additions to the structure concept of traditional C are found in this example: (1) it has members that are functions, such as assign, and (2) it has both public and private members. The keyword public indicates the visibility of the members that follow it. Without this keyword the members are private to the class. Private members are available for use only by other member functions of the class. Public members are available to any function within the scope of the class declaration. Privacy allows part of the implementation of a class type to be "hidden." This restriction prevents unanticipated modifications to the data structure. Restricted access or *data hiding* is a feature of object-oriented programming.

The declaration of member functions allows the ADT to have particular functions act on its private representation. For example, the member function length returns the length of the string defined to be the number of characters up to but excluding the first zero value character. The member function print outputs both the string and its length. The member function assign stores a character string into the hidden variable s and computes and stores its length in the hidden variable len.

We can now use this data type string as if it were a basic type of the language. It obeys the standard block structure scope rules of C.

Other code that uses this type is a *client*. The client can use the public members only to act on objects of type string.

```
//Test of the class string.
main()
{
    string   one, two;
    static char three[40] = {"My name is Charles Babbage."};

    one.assign("My name is Alan Turing.");
    two.assign(three);
    cout << three;
    cout << "\nLength: " << strlen(three) << "\n";
    //Print shorter of one and two.
    if (one.length() <= two.length())
        one.print();
    else
        two.print();
}
```

The variables one and two are of type string. The variable three is of type pointer to char and is not compatible with string. The member functions are called using the dot operator or "structure member operator." As is seen from their definitions, these member functions act on the hidden private member fields of the named variables. One cannot write inside main the expression one.len expecting to access this member. The output of this example program is

```
My name is Charles Babbage.
Length: 27
My name is Alan Turing.
Length: 23
```

Note, where there is full conformance to the ANSI C standard, auto aggregate initialization is allowed. In this example, the array three[] would not need to be declared static for it to be initialized. We retain static in our examples in this text for compatibility with systems not implementing this feature.

1.5. Overloading

The term *overloading* refers to the practice of giving several meanings
to an operator or a function. The meaning selected depends on the types
of the arguments used by the operator or function. Let us overload the
function print in the previous example. This will be a second definition
of the print function.

```
void print(char* c)
{
    cout << c << "\nLength is " << strlen(c) << "\n";
}
```

This version of print takes a single argument of type pointer to
char. Unlike the original version, it is not a member function. We can
modify main by deleting the two lines

```
cout << three;
cout << "\nLength: " << strlen(three) << "\n";
```

from the previous example and replacing them with a call to print:

```
print(three);
```

It is also possible to overload most of the standard C operators.
For example, let us overload + to mean concatenate two strings. To do
this we need to introduce two new keywords: friend and operator. The
keyword operator introduces the operator token and replaces what would
otherwise be a function name in a function declaration. The keyword
friend gives a function access to the private members of a class variable.
A friend function is not a member of the class, but has the privileges
of a member function in the class in which it is declared.

```
//Overloading the function print and the operator + .

#include <string.h>
#include <stream.h>

const int max_len = 255;

class string {
   char s[max_len];
   int  len;
public:
   void assign(char* st) { strcpy(s, st); len = strlen(st); }
   int  length() { return (len); }
   void print() { cout << s << "\nLength: " << len << "\n"; }
   friend string operator +(string& a, string& b);
};

string operator +(string& a, string& b)    //overload +
{
   string temp;

   temp.assign(a.s);
   if (a.len + b.len < max_len)
      temp.assign(strcat(temp.s, b.s));
   else
      cerr << "Max length exceeded in concatenation. \n";
   return (temp);
}

void print(char* c)
{
   cout << c << "\nLength: " << strlen(c) << "\n";
}
```

```
main()
{
    string      one, two, both;
    static char three[40] = {"My name is Charles Babbage."};

    one.assign("My name is Alan Turing.");
    two.assign(three);
    print(three);            //one form of print
    //Print shorter of one and two.
    if (one.length() <= two.length())
        one.print();         //member function form of print
    else
        two.print();
    both = one + two;        //plus overloaded to be concatenate
    both.print();
}
```

■ DISSECTION OF THE *operator* + FUNCTION

```
string operator +(string& a, string& b)
```

- Plus is overloaded. The two arguments it will take are both strings. The arguments are "called by reference." The declaration *type& identifier* declares the identifier to be a reference variable. This extension to traditional C allows call-by-reference as found in languages such as Pascal.

```
string temp;
```

- The function needs to return a value of type `string`. This local variable will be used to store and return the concatenated string value.

```
temp.assign(a.s);
if (a.len + b.len < max_len)
    temp.assign(temp.s, b.s);
```

- The string `a.s` is copied into `temp.s` by calling the `strcpy` library function. The length of the resulting concatenated string is tested to see that it does not exceed the maximum

length for strings. If the length is acceptable, the standard
library function `strcat` is called with the hidden string
members `temp.s` and `b.s`. The references to `temp.s`, `a.s`,
and `b.s` are allowed because this function is a `friend` of
class `string`.

```
cerr << "Max length exceeded in concatenation.\n";
```

- The standard error stream `cerr` is used to print an error
  message, and no concatenation takes place. Only the first
  string will be returned.

```
return (temp);
```

- The operator was given a return type of `string`, and `temp`
  has been assigned the appropriate concatenated string.

1.6. Constructors and Destructors

A constructor is a member function whose job is to initialize a variable
of its class. Such a variable is an *object*. In many cases this involves
dynamic storage allocation. A constructor is invoked anytime an object
of its associated class is created, typically when a variable is declared.
A destructor is a member function whose job is to deallocate a variable
of its class. Where an object has been allocated dynamically, its associated memory can be deallocated (returned to free store) by a destructor.
This is done by implicitly invoking the destructor upon block exit for
any class variables declared inside the block.

Let us change our `string` example by dynamically allocating store
for each `string` variable. We will replace the private array variable by a
pointer. The remodeled class will use a constructor to allocate an appropriate amount of storage dynamically using the `new` operator.

```
//An implementation of dynamically allocated strings.

class string {
    char* s;
    int   len;
public:
    string(int n) { s = new  char[n + 1]; len = n; }
    void assign(char* st) {  strcpy(s, st); len = strlen(st); }
    int  length() { return  (len); }
    void print() { cout << s << "\nLength: " << len << "\n"; }
    friend string operator + (string& a, string& b);
};
```

A constructor is a member function whose name is the same as the class name. The keyword new is an addition to the C language. It is a unary operator that takes as an argument a data type that can include an array size. It allocates the appropriate amount of memory to store this type from free store and returns the pointer value that addresses this memory. In the preceding example, n + 1 bytes would be allocated from free store. Thus the declaration

```
    string a(40), b(100);
```

would allocate 41 bytes for the variable a, pointed at by a.s, and 101 bytes for the variable b, pointed at by b.s. We add one byte for the end-of-string value 0. Storage obtained by new is persistent and is not automatically returned on block exit. When storage return is desired, a destructor function must be included in the class. A destructor is written as an ordinary member function whose name is the same as the class name preceded by the tilde symbol ~. Typically, a destructor uses the unary operator delete, another addition to the language, to automatically deallocate storage associated with a pointer expression.

```
    //Add as a member function to class string.
    ~string() { delete s; } //destructor
```

It is usual to overload the constructor, writing a variety of such functions to accommodate more than one style of initialization. Consider wanting to initialize a string with a pointer to char value. Such a constructor is

```
string(char* p)
{
    len = strlen(p);
    s = new char[len + 1];
    strcpy(s, p);
}
```

A typical declaration invoking this version of the constructor is

```
char*   str = "I came on foot.";
string  a("I came by bus."), b(str);
```

It would also be desirable to have a constructor of no arguments:

```
string() { len = 255; s = new char[255]; }
```

This would be invoked by declarations without parenthesized arguments and would, by default, allocate 255 bytes of memory. Now all three constructors would be invoked in the following declaration:

```
string  a, b(10), c("I came by horse.");
```

The overloaded constructor is selected by the form of each declaration. The variable a has no parameters and so is allocated 255 bytes. The variable b has an integer parameter and so is allocated 11 bytes. The variable c has a pointer parameter to the literal string "I came by horse." and so is allocated 17 bytes, with this literal string copied into its private s member.

1.7. Object-Oriented Programming and Inheritance

The central element of OOP is the encapsulation of an appropriate set of data types and their operations. The class construct with its member functions and data members provides an appropriate coding tool. Class variables are the *objects* to be manipulated.

Classes also provide data hiding. Access privileges can be managed and limited to whatever group of functions needs access to implementation details. This promotes modularity and robustness.

Another important concept in OOP is the promotion of code reuse through the *inheritance* mechanism. This is the mechanism of *deriving* a new class from an existing one called the *base* class. The base class can be added to or altered to create the derived class. In this way a hierarchy of related data types can be created that share code.

Many useful data structures are variants of one another, and it is frequently tedious to produce the same code for each. A derived class inherits the description of the base class. It can then be altered by adding members, overloading existing member functions, and modifying access privileges. Without this reuse mechanism, each minor variation would require code replication.

We will imagine that a stockbroker gets in a series of orders that are transactions. There will be different types of transactions. One type will be to buy or sell a stock. A second type will be to buy or sell a call on a stock. A call is an agreement that allows its holder to purchase a stock at an agreed to *strike-price* for a fixed length of time.

In this example we will code a base class `transact`. This class will have information common to subtypes, called `stock` and `call`, that are derived from it. These types inherit the `public` members of the base class. In OOP the types the user defines correspond to natural parts of the problem domain.

In `transact` there is a `virtual` function `profit_loss`. This function is overloaded in the derived class `stock`. These functions allow for dynamic or run-time typing. A pointer to the base class can also point at objects of the derived classes. When such a pointer is used to point at the overloaded virtual function, it dynamically selects which version of the member function to call. This is a difficult point that will be explained in detail in Chapter 6.

```
//Manipulating transactions using inheritance

#include <stream.h>

struct transact {        //base class for stock and call
   char     security[20];
   int      p_buy;
   int      p_sell;
   virtual int profit_loss() { return (p_sell - p_buy); }
};

//derived classes
class stock : public transact {
public:
   int   dividend;
   int   profit_loss() { return (dividend + p_sell - p_buy); }
};

class call : public transact {
public:
   int   strike_price;
   int   month;
};

main()
{
   transact* t[2];         //pointers to the base class
   stock     s;
   call      c;

   s.p_buy = 10;
   s.p_sell = 11;
   s.dividend = 2;
   c.p_buy = 10;
   c.p_sell = 11;

   t[0] = &s;              //a base class pointer can
   t[1] = &c;              //point at a derived class

   //the version of profit_loss selected corresponds
   //to the type of the object pointed at
   cout << t[0] -> profit_loss() << "\n";
   cout << t[1] -> profit_loss() << "\n";
}
```

Code reuse is achieved through inheritance. The derived classes `stock` and `call` have their own data members `security[20]`, `p_buy`, and `p_sell` inherited from `transact`. It is easy to modularly extend this code to other transaction categories, such as bonds and puts. Inheritance creates a type hierarchy that can be used dynamically with `virtual` functions.

The OOP programming task is frequently more difficult than normal procedural programming as found in C. There is at least one extra design step before one gets to the coding of algorithms. This involves the hierarchy of types that is useful for the problem at hand. Frequently one is solving the problem more generally than is strictly necessary.

The belief is that this will pay dividends in several ways. The solution will be more encapsulated and thus more robust and easier to maintain and change. Also, the solution will be more reusable. For example, where the code needs a stack, that stack is easily borrowed from existing code. In an ordinary procedural language, such a data structure is frequently "wired into" the algorithm and cannot be exported.

All these benefits are especially important for large coding projects that require coordination among many programmers. Here the ability to have header files specify general interfaces for different classes allows each programmer to work on individual code segments with a high degree of independence and integrity.

1.8. Summary

1. The double slash `//` is a new comment symbol. The comment runs to the end of the line. The old C bracketing comment symbols `/* */` are still available for multiline comments.

2. The *stream.h* header introduces I/O facilities for C++. The identifier `cout` is the name of the standard output stream. The operator `<<` passes its argument to standard out. Used in this way, the `<<` is referred to as the *put to* or *insertion* operator.

3. The identifier `cin` is the name of the standard input stream. The *input operator* `>>` is called the *get from* or *extraction* operator that assigns values from the input stream to a variable.

4. C++ reduces C's traditional reliance on the preprocessor. Instead of using `define`, special constants are assigned to variables specified

as `const`. The new keyword `inline` specifies that a function is to be compiled, if possible as a macro. As a rule, this should be done sparingly and only on short functions.

5. The syntax of functions in C++ inspired the new function proto-type syntax found in ANSI C compilers. Basically, the types of parameters are listed inside the header parentheses, for example `int add3(int, int, int)`. By explicitly listing the type and number of arguments, strong type checking and assignment-compatible conversions are possible in C++.

6. What is truly novel about C++ is the aggregate type `class`, which is introduced by the language. A `class` is an extension of the idea of `struct` in traditional C. Its use is a way of implementing a data type and associated functions and operators. Therefore a `class` is an implementation of an abstract data type (ADT). There are two important additions to the structure concept: (1) it includes members that are functions and (2) it employs a new keyword, `public`. This keyword indicates the visibility of the members that follow it. Without this keyword, the members are private to the class. Private members are available for use only by other member functions of the class. Public members are available to any function within the scope of the class declaration. Privacy allows part of the implementation of a class type to be "hidden."

7. The term *overloading* refers to the practice of giving several meanings to an operator or a function. The meaning selected will depend on the types of the arguments used by the operator or function.

8. The keyword `operator` introduces the operator token and replaces what would otherwise be a function name in a function declaration. The keyword `friend` gives a function access to the private members of a class variable. A `friend` function is not a member of the class, but has the privileges of a member function in the class in which it is declared.

9. A constructor is a member function whose job is to initialize a variable of its class. In many cases this involves dynamic storage allocation. Constructors are invoked anytime an object of its associated class is created, typically when a variable is declared.

10. A destructor is a member function whose job is to deallocate a variable of its class. Where an object has been allocated dynami-

cally, its associated memory can be deallocated (returned to free store) by a destructor. This is done by implicitly invoking the destructor upon block exit for any class variables declared inside the block.

11. The central element of object-oriented programming (OOP) is the encapsulation of an appropriate set of data types and their operations. These user-defined types are ADTs. The class construct with its member functions and data members provides an appropriate coding tool. Class variables are the *objects* to be manipulated.

12. Another important concept in OOP is the promotion of code reuse through the *inheritance* mechanism. This is the mechanism of *deriving* a new class from an existing one called the *base* class. The base class can be added to or altered to create the derived class. In this way a hierarchy of related data types can be created that share code. This typing hierarchy can be used dynamically by `virtual` functions. Virtual member functions in a base class are overloaded in a derived class. These functions allow for dynamic or run-time typing. A pointer to the base class can also point at objects of the derived classes. When such a pointer is used to point at the overloaded virtual function, it dynamically selects which version of the member function to call.

1.9. Exercises

1. Using stream I/O, write on the screen the words

```
she sells sea shells by the seashore
```

   (a) all on one line, (b) on three lines, (c) inside a box.

2. Write a program that will convert distances measured in yards to distances measured in meters. The relationship is 1 meter equals 1.0936 yards. Write the program to use `cin` to read in distances. The program should be a loop that does this calculation until it receives a zero or negative number for input.

3. The CC compiler will complain about the file not ending in ".*c*". On some systems the complaint is quite cryptic. See what error message you get by attempting to compile a file not ending in ".*c*".

4. Take a working program, omit each line in turn, and run it through
   the compiler. Record the error messages each such deletion causes.
   For example use the following code:

```
#include <stream.h>

main()
{
    int  m, n, k;
    cout << "\nEnter two integers: ";
    cin  >> m >> n;
    k = m + n;
    cout << "\nTheir sum is " << k << ".\n";
}
```

5. The text editor *vi* provides several facilities to help in writing code.
   For example, when the cursor is sitting on a { character, typing the
   % key causes the cursor to go to the matching brace symbol, if there
   is one. This facility allows you to conveniently check if your left
   and right braces are properly matched. It works in a similar fashion
   for brackets and parentheses. If *vi* is available to you, check this
   feature. Also, find out how to set and make use of "autoindent" and
   "showmatch" in *vi*. If you are using some other text editor, find out
   what special features, if any, the editor provides to help you write
   code.

6. Write a program that asks interactively for your *name* and *age* and
   responds with

```
Hello name, next year you will be next_age.
```

   where *next_age* is *age* + 1 .

7. Stream I/O also allows formatted output using the function form().
   The function prototype is

```
char* form(const char* format, ...);
//... denotes a variable number of arguments
```

   Here are some examples of its use:

```
cout << form("\nThe value of i = %d\n", i);
cout << form("%f %f %f", x, y, z);
cout << form("%10.4f %4d %5c", x, i, 'c');
```

It mimics `printf()` in traditional C, and it respects the same format symbols and conversion characters.

Write a program using `form()` to print out a table whose entries are:

```
i       i * i      square root      i * i * i
------------------------------------------------
1           1      1.00000                 1
. . .
```

This topic is covered in detail in Section 7.2.

8. The traditional C swapping function is

```
void swap(i, j)
int*   i;
int*   j;
{
    int   temp;

    temp = *i;
    *i = *j;
    *j = temp;
}
```

Rewrite this using reference parameters and test it.

```
void swap(int& i, int& j)
. . .
```

9. In traditional C, the following code causes an error:

```
#include <math.h>

main()
{
    printf("%f is the square root of 2.\n", sqrt(2));
}
```

Explain the reason for this and why function prototypes in C++ avoid this problem. Rewrite in C++.

10. Add to the `class string` a member function `reverse`. This function reverses the underlying representation of the character sequence stored in the private member `s`.

11. Add to the class string a member function void print (int k). This function overloads print () and is meant to print the first k characters of the string.

12. Overload the operator * in class string. Its member declaration will be

```
string operator *(string& a, int n);
```

The string represented by a should be copied back into a n times. Check that this does not overrun storage.

13. Test your compiler on character output by running

```
#include <stream.h>

main()
{
    char  c = 'C';

    cout << c << ":" << chr(c) << ":"
              << dec(c, 6) << ":"
              << form("%c", c) << "\n";
}
```

On some systems the first value printed will be 67. The special format functions chr and dec force the integer-valued expression to be printed as char and int, respectively. For a more extensive discussion of this topic see Chapter 7.

14. The first CC compiler, as written by Bjarne Stroustrup of Bell Laboratories, is based on a compiler *cfront*, which generates C code. It then invokes the regular C compiler *cc* to produce executable code. On these systems it is possible to generate and save the C code. Read the online manual for CC and run the option that produces C code. Try it on a program in this chapter.

CHAPTER 2

C++ as a Better C

C++ extends the C programming language in a number of important ways. Its new features make it more reliable and easier to use than traditional C. Many of these features are independent of the additions connected to the `class` construct. This chapter describes these improvements. Its theme is that C++ can be used as an improved and better C.

Some of the changes described are minor though useful. Among these is the new comment style. Some of the changes are major, such as function prototypes, which have been adopted into the ANSI C standard. There are also changes in the type compatibility rules. These are stronger in C++, and the compiler provides much of the checking that is relegated to *lint* in traditional C.

Several features of C++ affect type declarations. These include the use of `void`, `void*`, `enum`, and `const`, all unavailable in traditional C, but adopted in more recent compilers and in the ANSI C standard. They also include the use of the keyword `inline` for function declarations and the use of `&` to mean the declaration is reference to. All these changes will be explained with examples.

In this chapter, then, we discuss the new comment style, the use of the keywords `const` and `inline`, the uses of the `void` and `void*` type, the function prototype construct, the use of reference declarations, the overloading of functions, and the use of the free store operators `new` and `delete`.

2.1. Comment Style

Programs must be documented to be useful. C++ introduces a one-line comment symbol `//`. This is in addition to the bracket pair comment symbols `/* */` of traditional C. Everything on a single line after the symbol `//` is treated as a comment. This is even the case when the symbol appears in a string, which is not true for bracket pair comments. The one-line comment symbol is the preferred C++ style. In general it is less error prone—bracket pair symbols can cause problems, for example, when one of the pair is omitted.

```
//The computation of circumference and area of circles.
//                   by
//             Geometrics Inc.
//             Version 2.2

#include <stream.h>

const  float pi = 3.14159;      //pi accurate to six places
const  int true = 1;            //mnemonic identifier

inline float circum(float rad) { return (pi * 2 * rad); }
inline float area(float rad) { return (pi * rad * rad); }

main()
{
    float  r;

    while (true) {                     //exit with control-C
       cout << "\nEnter radius: ";     //prompt for input
       cin >> r;
       cout << "\nArea is " << area(r);
       cout << "\nCircumference is " << circum(r) << "\n";
    }
}
```

2.2. Avoiding the Preprocessor: inline and const

In the previous example and in examples in Chapter 1, the new keywords inline and const are used to avoid the use of the preprocessor define. Using the preprocessor to define macros has a clear drawback: namely, the preprocessor does not understand C syntax. For example:

```
#define SQ(X)    X * X
```

expands the code

```
SQ(a + b)
```

to

```
a + b * a + b
```

This problem is avoided by fully parenthesizing the original macro. However, the solution does not protect against improper types being used. This latter defect is remedied by using `inline`.

```
inline int SQ(int x) { return (x * x); }
```

The keyword `inline` is a request to the compiler that the function be compiled as a macro. The compiler may choose to ignore this suggestion, but either way the semantics are identical. Only very short functions, where function call overhead is an issue, should use this function specifier.

The `const` keyword is a type specifier. When used alone in a declaration, the base type is implicity `int`. A variable declared as `const` cannot have its value changed. Thus a `const` variable cannot be used on the left-hand side of an assignment. A non-`const` variable can have its value changed. It is a modifiable *lvalue*. An lvalue is an expression that refers to an object, typically a reference to a variable. A `const` variable should also be initialized. As in the previous program, it is used to create named constants, an important documentation aid. Some examples are

```
const   false = 0;               //implicit type is int
const   double e = 2.71828;      //natural logarithm base
const   int M_size = 100;        //used in an array declaration
const* p = &M_size;              //a pointer to a constant int
char*   const s = "abcde";       //a constant pointer to char
```

Some care needs to be taken with respect to constant declarations of pointer types. The distinction is between the form

```
const type* identifier
```

which declares the *identifier* as a pointer whose pointed at value is constant, and the form

```
type* const identifier
```

which declares the *identifier* as a pointer constant. So,

```
const int* const cp = &M_size;
```

declares cp to be a constant pointer whose pointed at value is constant.

2.3. Declarations

This section describes changes to declarations in C++. It discusses the meaning of enum and illustrates the fact that declarations can be inter-mixed with executable statements. It also explains that the struct tag name and enum tag name are types.

We will write a card shuffling program to illustrate these points. First we define a card as a struct.

```
enum suit {clubs, diamonds, hearts, spades};

struct card {
    suit   s;
    int    pips;
};

card deck[52];     //a declaration using card as the type
```

In traditional C, the declaration of deck would be illegal. It would have to be

```
enum suit {clubs, diamonds, hearts, spades};

struct card {
    enum suit   s;
    int         pips;
};

struct card deck[52];
```

In C++, the tag names are types.

Enumerated types were added to C compilers in the early 1980s. Frequently they were implemented with a variety of underlying seman-tics. C++ treats enumerated types as integer variables, in accord with ANSI C. When listed without initialized values, the identifiers in the enumerated lists are implicitly initialized consecutively starting with 0. These identifiers are named integer constants and may not be changed. So, the two declarations

```
enum suit {clubs, diamonds, hearts, spades};
enum suit {clubs = 0, diamonds = 1, hearts = 2, spades = 3};
```

are equivalent, as are

```
enum suit {clubs = 5, diamonds, hearts, spades = 3};
enum suit {clubs = 5, diamonds = 6, hearts = 7, spades = 3};
```

As we saw in Chapter 1, C++ allows declarations to be intermixed with executable statements. Consider a function that initializes a deck of cards to the normal 52 card values.

```
void init_deck(card d[])
{
   for (int i = 0; i < 52; ++i) {
      d[i].s = (i/13);              //enum is an int
      d[i].pips = 1 + i % 13;
   }
}
```

In this function the declaration int i occurs inside the for statement parentheses. The scope of the declaration is the innermost block within which it is found, and the identifier is visible starting at the point at which it is declared. Otherwise the scope rules are the same as in C, which means that declarations can be readily placed near their use.

The program for deck shuffling follows.

```
//  Shuffling a card deck

#include <stream.h>

int  random(void);                    // standard library function

enum suit {clubs, diamonds, hearts, spades};

struct card {
    suit   s;
    int    pips;
};

void pr_card(card cd)
{
    switch (cd.pips)  {
        case 1 :   cout << "A"; break;
        case 11:   cout << "J"; break;
        case 12:   cout << "Q"; break;
        case 13:   cout << "K"; break;
        default:   cout << cd.pips;
    }
    switch (cd.s)  {
        case clubs:     cout << "C"; break;
        case diamonds:  cout << "D"; break;
        case hearts:    cout << "H"; break;
        case spades:    cout << "S"; break;
        default :       cerr << "suit error\n"; exit(1);
    }
    cout << "  ";
}


void init_deck(card d[])
{
    for (int i = 0; i < 52; ++i) {
        d[i].s = (i/13);                  //enum is an int
        d[i].pips = 1 + i % 13;
    }
}
```

Most interesting, however, is the use of void∗ as a generic pointer type. This type is also in the ANSI C standard. A pointer declared as type pointer to void, as in void∗ gp, can be assigned a pointer value of any underlying base type. But it may not be dereferenced. Dereferencing is the operation ∗ acting on a pointer value to obtain what is pointed at. It would not make sense to dereference a pointer to a void value. Therefore

```
void* gp;       //generic pointer
int*  ip;       //int pointer
char* cp;       //char pointer

gp = ip;            //legal conversion
ip = (int*) gp;     //legal conversion
cp = ip;            //illegal conversion
*ip = 15;           //legal dereferencing of a pointer to int
*ip = *gp;          //illegal dereferencing of a generic pointer
```

A key use for this type is as a formal parameter. For example, the library function memcpy is declared in string.h as

```
void* memcpy(void* s1, const void* s2, unsigned int n);
```

This function copies n characters from the object based at s2 into the object based at s1. It works with any two pointer types as actual arguments.

2.5. Scope Resolution Operator ::

C is a block-structured language. C++ inherits the same notions of block and scope. In such languages, the same identifier can be used to mean different objects. A use in an inner block *hides* the outer block or external use of the same name. C++ introduces the operator :: called the scope resolution operator. When used in the form :: *variable*, it allows access to the externally named variable. As in the following example, it is assumed that this uncovers an otherwise hidden object. Beware! Because it breaks the modularity of the code, this is a dangerous practice that is rarely justified.

```
//  ::   scope resolution operator

int i = 1;                    //external i

#include    <stream.h>

main()
{
   int    i = 2;              //redeclares i locally

   {
      cout << "enter inner block\n";
      int  n = i;             //the global i is still visible
      int  i = 3;             //hides the global i

      //print the local i and the external i
      cout << i  << "  i <> ::i  " << ::i << "\n";
      cout << "n = " << n << "\n";
   }
   cout << "enter outer block\n";
   cout << i  << "  i <> ::i  " << ::i << "\n";
}
```

The output of this code is

```
enter inner block
3  i <> ::i  1
n = 2
enter outer block
2  i <> ::i  1
```

The major uses of this notation are important for classes. They will be
discussed in the next chapters.

2.6. Function Prototypes

The single feature in C++ that most accounts for its greater reliability
over traditional C is its use of function prototypes. By explicitly listing
the type and number of arguments, strong type checking and assignment-
compatible conversions are possible in C++. The success of this feature
inspired ANSI C to adopt it.

In traditional C, a function may be declared before it is defined, with the form

   type name ();

This declaration announces that the function is defined elsewhere with the given `return` type. However, the compiler makes no assumptions about type and number of arguments. Therefore, in traditional C, when a function is invoked with an actual argument, the explicit value of that argument is passed as is, without being converted to the defined function's corresponding argument type. A most common error occurs when functions such as `sqrt` are passed `int` valued expressions.

```
printf("%f is sqrt of 4\n", sqrt(4));
```

This prints 0 on many traditional C systems. The function `sqrt` expects a `double`, and the bit configuration for the `int` constant 4, when interpreted as `double`, passes `sqrt` an argument whose value is 0.

In C++ the prototype form is

   type name (*argument-declaration-list*);

Examples are:

```
double  sqrt(double x);
void    pr_int(char*, int);        //definition contains names
void    ring_bell(void);           //function of no arguments
int     printf(char* format, ...); //variable no. of args.
```

With the above `sqrt` prototype definition, the call to

```
sqrt(4)
```

causes a conversion from `int` value 4 to `double` value 4 to occur before the function call is executed. The argument-declaration-list can either have named arguments or omit them. These names are intended as possible documentation. It is not necessary, but it is good style for names in prototype declarations to match names used in the actual definition. The prototype for the `stdio.h` function `printf` has an ellipsis ". . ." that is used to specify that the function argument list has unknown length and type.

The following example illustrates these points.

```
//Compute the average of a set of int values.

#include <stream.h>

int data[10] = {99, 87, 67, 90, 66, 43, 89, 88, 97, 76};

main()
{
   void    pr_arr(char*, int*, int);
   void    pr_dbl(char* name, double x);
   double avg_arr(int a[], int size);

   pr_arr("data", data, 10);
   pr_dbl("average", avg_arr(data, 10));
}

void pr_int(char* name, int k)
{
   cout << form("%s = ", name) << k << "\n";
}

void pr_dbl(char* name, double x)
{
   cout << form("%s = ", name) << x << "\n";
}

void pr_arr(char* name, int a[], int size)
{
   cout << name ;
   pr_int(" array, size ", size);
   for (int i = 0; i < size; ++i)
      cout << a[i] << "\t";
   cout << "\n";
}

double avg_arr(int a[], int size)    //compute average
{
   int   sum = 0;

   for (int i = 0; i < size; ++i)
      sum += a[i];
   return ((double) sum / size);
}
```

The output from this program is

```
data array, size  = 10
99     87    67     90    66    43    89    88    97    76
average = 80.2
```

The program uses the *stream.h* library function form to provide formatted output. This function is described in detail in Section 7.2.

2.7. Call-by-Reference and Reference Declarations

C++ allows *reference to* declarations. These are typically of the form

   type& identifier = object

Such declarations declare the identifier to be an alternative name for an object specified in an initialization of the reference. Some examples are

```
int     n;
int&    nn = n;            //nn is an alternative name for n
double  a[10];
double& last = a[9];       //last is an alias for a[9]
char&   new_line = '\n';
```

In these examples, the names n and nn are aliases for each other; that is, they refer to the same object. Modifying nn is equivalent to modifying n and vice versa. The name last is an alternative to the single array element a[9]. These names, once initialized, cannot be changed. Also, it is possible to initialize a reference to a literal. In the examples, new_line is initialized to the char constant \n, which creates a reference to the otherwise unknown location where the literal is stored.

The chief use of reference declarations is in formal parameter lists. This usage allows C++ to have *call-by-reference* arguments directly. Let us use this mechanism to write a function greater that exchanges two values if the first is greater than the second.

```
int greater(int& a, int& b)
{
   if (a > b) {              //exchange
      int temp = a;
      a = b;
      b = temp;
      return (1);
   }
   else
      return (0);
}
```

Now, if i and j are two int variables, then

```
greater(i, j)
```

will use the reference to i and the reference to j to exchange, if necessary, their two values. In traditional C, this operation must be accomplished using pointers and dereferencing.

2.8. Default Arguments

A formal parameter can be given a default argument. This is usually a constant that occurs frequently when the function is called. Use of a default argument saves writing in this default value at each invocation. The following function illustrates the point.

```
int mult(int n, int k = 2)          //k = 2 is default
{
   if (k == 2)
      return (n * n);
   else
      return (mult(n, k - 1) * n);
}
```

We assume that most of the time the function is used to return the value of n squared.

```
mult(i + 5)                 //computes (i + 5) * (i + 5)
mult(i + 5, 3)              //computes (i + 5) cubed
```

Only the trailing parameters of a function can have default values. Some examples are

```
void foo(int i, int j = 7);                //legal
void goo(int i = 3, int j);                //illegal
void hoo(int i, int j = 3, int k = 7);     //legal
void moo(int i = 1, int j = 2, int k = 3); //legal
void noo(int i, int j = 2, int k);         //illegal
```

2.9. Overloading Functions

The term *overloading* refers to using the same name for multiple meanings of an operator or a function. The meaning selected depends on the types of the arguments used by the operator or function. C++ introduces the keyword `overload` to indicate that a particular name will be so used. This keyword is no longer necessary, but can be used in declarations of type function. Here we will restrict our discussion to function overloading and leave operator overloading to later chapters, as the latter is chiefly used in the context of classes.

The usual reason for picking a function name is to indicate the function's chief purpose. Readable programs generally have a diverse and literate choice of identifiers. Sometimes different functions are used for the same purpose. For example, consider a function that averages the values in an array of `double` versus one that averages the values in an array of `int`. Both are conveniently named `avg_arr`, as in a previous example.

```
overload avg_arr; //an anachronism
double avg_arr(double a[], int size);
double avg_arr(int a[], int size);

double avg_arr(int a[], int size)
{
   int  sum = 0;

   for (int i = 0; i < size; ++i)
      sum += a[i];                    //performs int arithmetic
   return ((double) sum / size);
}
```

```
double avg_arr(double a[], int size)
{
    double  sum = 0.0;

    for (int i = 0; i < size; ++i)
        sum += a[i];                    //performs double arithmetic
    return (sum / size);
}
```

The following code shows how each is invoked:

```
main()
{
    static int    w[5] = {1, 2, 3, 4, 5};
    static double x[5] = {1.1, 2.2, 3.3, 4.4, 5.5};

    cout << avg_arr(w, 5) << "  int array average\n";
    cout << avg_arr(x, 5) << "  double array average\n";
}
```

The compiler chooses the function with matching types and arguments.

2.10. Free Store Operators new and delete

The unary operators new and delete are available to manipulate *free store*. They are more convenient than and can be used to replace the standard library functions malloc, calloc, and free in many applications. Free store is a system-provided memory pool for objects whose lifetime is directly managed by the programmer. The programmer creates the object by using new and destroys the object by using delete. This is important for dynamic data structures such as lists and trees.

The operator new is used in the following forms:

new *type-name*
new *type-name initializer*
new (*type-name*)

In each case there are minimally two effects. First, an appropriate amount of store is allocated from free store to contain the named type. Second, the base address of the object is returned as the value of the new expression. The expression is a pointer value and can be assigned to that pointer type variable. The use of the operator with initializer, which applies to its use with classes, is not discussed here.

The following example uses new:

```
int* i;
i = new int;
*i = 5;
```

In this code, the pointer to int variable i is assigned the address of the store obtained in allocating an object of type int. The pointer is dereferenced and assigned the value 5. This use is not usual for a simple type such as int in that it is far more convenient and natural to automatically allocate an integer variable on the stack or globally.

The operator delete destroys an object created by new, in effect returning its allocated storage to free store for reuse. The following example uses these constructs to dynamically allocate an array:

```
//Use of new operator to dynamically allocate an array.

#include <stream.h>

main()
{
    int*    data;
    int     size;

    cout << "\nEnter array size: ";
    cin >> size;

    data = new int[size];
    for (int j = 0; j < size; ++j)
        cout << (data[j] = j) << "\t";
    cout << "\n\n";

    delete data;
    data = new int[size];
    for (j = 0; j < size; ++j)
        cout << data[j] << "\t";
}
```

■ DISSECTION OF THE *dynamic* PROGRAM

```
int*   data;
int    size;

cout << "\nEnter array size: ";
cin >> size;

data = new int[size];
```

- The pointer variable `data` is used as the base address of a dynamically allocated array whose number of elements is the value of `size`. The user is prompted for the integer-valued `size`. The `new` operator is used to allocate storage from free store capable of storing an object of type `int[size]`. On a system where integers take 4 bytes, this would allocate 4 * `size` bytes. At this point `data` is assigned the base address of this store.

```
for (int j = 0; j < size; ++j)
   cout << (data[j] = j) << "\t";
```

- This statement initializes the values of the `data` array and prints them.

```
delete data;
```

- The operator `delete` returns the storage associated with the pointer variable `data` to free store. This can be done only with objects allocated by `new`.

```
data = new int[size];
for (j = 0; j < size; ++j)
   cout << data[j] << "\t";
```

- We access free store again, but this time do not initialize the `data` array. On a typical system, the same memory just returned to free store is used, with the old values reappearing. However, there are no guarantees on what values will appear in objects allocated from free store. Test this on your system. The programmer is responsible for properly initializing such objects.

■

The operator `delete` is used in the following forms:

```
delete expression
delete [ expression ] expression
```

The first form is the most common. The expression is typically a pointer variable used in a previous `new` expression. The second form is occasionally used when returning store that was allocated as an array type. The bracketed expression gives the number of elements of the array. The operator `delete` does not return a value. Equivalently, one can say its return type is `void`.

2.11. Odds and Ends

Several other features of C++ that do not appear in traditional C are relatively minor. Among these are the use of `signed`, the treatment of `float`, and the use of anonymous unions. We will treat these matters briefly.

The ANSI C standard introduces the keyword `signed`, which is analogous to the keyword `unsigned`. The keywords `signed` and `unsigned` are type specifiers for the integral types. The `unsigned` type does not allow negative values while the `signed` type does. Recent C++ compilers have adopted this keyword and associated type conversion rules.

The type `float` in traditional C was always promoted to `double` when used in expressions. C++, however, reserves the right to do arithmetic in single precision `float`. Actual usage must be checked, though, as this is system-dependent.

An anonymous `union` is a `union` declared without a tag name. C++ allows the member names of such unions to be used directly, but they must be distinct from other identifiers defined within the same scope. A global anonymous union has to have storage class `static`. An example (run on a SUN) is:

```
//Anonymous Unions

#include <stream.h>

static union {
    int     i;
    char    c[4];
    double  w;
};

main()
{
    i = 65;
    cout << form("%c", c[3]) << "\n";
}
```

What gets printed is A. The low-order byte that is used by the integer member i to store the value 65 is accessed by the indexed character member c[3]. In a union the member declarations share the same storage. This technique is used to conserve storage and avoid unnecessary type conversions.

2.12. Summary

1. Programs must be documented to be useful. C++ introduces a one-line comment symbol //. This is in addition to the bracket pair comment symbols /* */ of traditional C. Everything on a single line after the symbol // is treated as a comment.

2. The keyword inline is a request to the compiler that the function be compiled as a macro. Only very short functions, where function

call overhead is an issue, should use this function specifier. The const keyword is a type specifier. When used alone in a declaration, the base type is implicitly int. A variable declared as const cannot have its value changed. It can be used in places that otherwise would require a literal, such as an array size. It cannot be used on the left-hand side of an assignment; thus, unlike a non-const variable, it is not an *lvalue*.

3. Enumerated types were added to C compilers in the early 1980s. C++ treats them as integer variables in accord with ANSI C. When listed without initialized values, the identifiers in the enumerated lists are implicitly initialized consecutively starting with 0. These identifiers are named integer constants and may not be changed.

4. The tag names of both enumerated and structure types can be used as type names. Declarations may be intermixed with executable statements.

5. The type void was introduced in some C compilers in the early 1980s. It is standard in ANSI C. It improves both documentation and type checking over traditional C. The keyword void is used as the return type of a function not returning a value as well as to indicate an empty argument list. Two further uses are as a cast, and as part of the type pointer to void.

6. C++ introduces the operator :: called the scope resolution operator. When used in the form :: *variable*, it allows access to the externally named variable.

7. The single feature in C++ that most accounts for its greater reliability over traditional C is its use of function prototypes. By explicitly listing the type and number of arguments, strong type checking and assignment-compatible conversions are possible in C++. In C++ the prototype form is

type name (*argument-declaration-list*) ;

Examples are:

```
double sqrt (double x) ;
void   pr_int (char*, int) ;      //definition contains names
void   ring_bell (void) ;         //function of no arguments
int    printf (char* format, ...) ;   //variable no. of args.
```

8. C++ allows *reference to* declarations. These are typically of the form

> *type&* *identifier* = *object*

These declare the identifier to be an alternative name for an object specified in an initialization of the reference. The chief use of reference declarations is in formal parameter lists. This allows C++ to have *call-by-reference* arguments.

9. A formal parameter can be given a default argument. This is usually a constant that occurs frequently when the function is called. Use of the default argument saves writing in this default value at each invocation.

10. The term *overloading* refers to using the same name for various meanings of an operator or a function. The meaning selected depends on the types of the arguments used by the operator or function. C++ introduces the keyword `overload` to indicate that a particular name will be so used. This keyword is no longer necessary, but can be used in declarations of type function.

11. The unary operators `new` and `delete` are available to manipulate *free store*. Free store is a system-provided memory pool for objects whose lifetime is directly managed by the programmer. The programmer creates the object by using `new` and destroys the object by using `delete`. The operator `new` is used in the following forms:

> `new` *type-name*
> `new` *type-name initializer*
> `new` *(type-name)*

The expression is of type `void*` and can be assigned to any pointer type variable.

2.13. Exercises

1. C++ style follows C style in layout. Generally a tab stop of three to five blank spaces is used to indent sections of code to reflect flow of control. Proper commenting and choice of identifier names are

important to readable code. Try to understand the following code and rewrite it in good style:

```
#include <stream.h>
const float f = 3.14159;
inline float v(float b) {return 4*f*b*b*b/3.0; }
main() {float b; while (1) { cout << "enter b"; cin >> b;
cout << form("\nVolume is %f \n", v(b)); }}
```

2. Can you have the following as comments in C and C++?

```
//one liner
/*one liner
/*    old style */
/*    is nesting /* allowed */ on your system? */
//what happens if we repeat // on this line
a /*p; where p is a pointer
"/* within a string */"
"// within a string"
//   /* within a one liner */
/*   //okay I give up   */
```

3. Recode the following #define preprocessor lines using const and inline declarations:

```
#define TRUE         1
#define c            299792.4562  //light speed in km/sec
#define EOF          (-1)
#define LARGER(X,Y)  ((X > Y) ? (X) : (Y))
#define CUBE(X)      (X) * (X) * (X)
```

4. Using the declaration of card deck[52] as found in this chapter, write code that will deal out and print six 5-card hands. A hand should be stored in a two-dimensional array

```
const int players = 6;
const int nc      = 5;
card  hand[players][nc];
```

5. Continuing with exercise 4 write code that checks if a hand is a flush. A flush is a hand that contains five or more cards of the same suit. It can be tested by summing for each suit the number of cards of that suit that occur. You will write the function

```
int is_flush(card h[]);   //returns 1 if a flush else 0
```

Generate 1000 deals at random and print out the probability of getting a flush.

6. On most C compilers the following program runs:

```
char strg[5] = "ABCD";

main()
{
    int  i = 7, *p = &i;
    char* c;

    c = *p;
    c = strg + 1;
    *c = 'X';
}
```

On C++ compilers the program gives a syntax error. Discuss these differences. Which is preferred?

7. The following program uses pointer types and modifies a string:

```
#include <stream.h>

main()
{
    char*           c;
    static char*  const strg = "ABCD";

    cout << "\nstrg is " << strg;
    c = strg + 1;
    *c = 'X';
    cout << "\n strg is " <<   strg;
}
```

What is wrong with changing the strg declaration to

```
static const char*  const strg = "ABCD";
```

8. Given the following declarations:

```
int    i = 5;
int*  pi = &i;
char   c = 'C';
char*  pc = &c;
void*  pv;
char   s[100];
```

what do the following expressions mean? Are any illegal under C++ typing?

```
*pi = i + c;
*pc = s + 10;
pc  = s + 10;
pv  = pi;
pv  = s + 1;
pv  = ++s;
pc  = pv;
*pc = *pv;
*pc = (char)*pv;
```

9. Use the library function `memcpy` to copy a string into another character array. Also copy an integer array into another integer array. Finally, copy a character array into an integer array. On most systems the header `string.h` has `memcpy`.

10. Implement your own version of `memcpy` to conform to the function prototype found in Section 2.4.

11. What gets printed by the following code?

```
//  ::  scope resolution operator

double x = 1.23;

#include    <stream.h>

main()
{
    double   x = 2.34;

    {
        double   y = x;
        double   x = 3.45;
        cout << x  << "   x <> ::x  " << ::x << "\n";
        cout << "y = " << y << "\n";
    }
    cout << x  << "   x <> ::x  " << ::x << "\n";
}
```

12. The following traditional C function uses pointer variables and dereferencing to implement a circular shift:

```
void shift(pc1, pc2, pc3, pc4)
char*   pc1;
char*   pc2;
char*   pc3;
char*   pc4;
{
    char   temp;

    temp = *pc1;
    *pc1 = *pc2;
    *pc2 = *pc3;
    *pc3 = *pc4;
    *pc4 = temp;
}
```

Convert it to a function in C++ using call-by-reference.

```
void shift(char& c1, char& c2, char& c3, char& c4)
```

Write a test program that prints the before and after values using shift.

13. The following function computes the minimum and maximum values found in an array:

```
//Find both the minimum and maximum values of an array.

void minmax(int data[], int size, int* min, int* max)
{
    *min = *max = data[0];
    for (int i = 1; i < size; ++i)
      if (*min > data[i])
        *min = data[i];
      else if (*max < data[i])
        *max = data[i];
}
```

Convert it to a function that uses call-by-reference. Write a program to test it.

14. A more efficient method for finding minimum and maximum is as follows. Compare a pair of elements and use the smaller element for finding the minimum and the larger element for finding the maximum. With this method, rewrite the function used in exercise 13. How many comparisons are saved over the previous method? A description of this method is found in "A Sorting Method and Its Complexity" by Ira Pohl (*Communications of the ACM*, Vol. 15, No. 6, 1972).

15. Change the solution to exercise 13 to use a default size parameter. Let the default value be 10. (Reminder: The argument size must now be at the end of the argument list.)

16. Write three overloaded functions that each print an array. One will print an array of int, the second an array of float, and the third an array of char.

```
overload print;
void print(int data[], int size = 20);    //int version
void print(float data[], int size = 20); //float version
void print(char data[], int size = 20);   //char version
```

Note that each declaration has a default value for size. Use stream I/O when writing each function.

17. First write a function that creates a vector of a user-keyed size and that reads in, using cin, its size and initial values.

```
void create_vec(int* &v, int& size);
//get array size from cin
//use new to create v[size]
//and then use a for loop to assign values from cin
```

Next write a function that will add two vectors. If the vectors are not the same size, add them for the lesser of the two sizes.

```
void add_vec(int* v1, int* v2, int* sum, int size);
//add_vec   returns vector sum    sum[i] = v1[i] + v2[i]
```

Finally, print out the resulting array.

```
void print_vec (int* v, int size);
```

18. The following code uses new to allocate a two-dimensional array:

```
//Dynamically allocated two dimensional arrays

#include <stream.h>

main()
{
    int**  data;
    int    sz1, sz2, i, j;

    cout << "\nEnter two sizes: ";
    cin >> sz1 >> sz2;
    data = new int* [sz1];              //an array of pointers
    for (i = 0; i < sz1; ++i)
        data[i] = new int[sz2];         //each row is allocated
    cout << "\nEnter " << sz1 << " by " << sz2 << " ints\n";
    for (i = 0; i < sz1; ++i)
        for (j = 0; j < sz2; ++j)
            cin >> data[i][j];
    for (i = 0; i < sz1; ++i)
        for (j = 0; j < sz2; ++j)
            cout << data[i][j] << "\t";
    cout << "\n";
}
```

Notice that you must do the allocation in two stages. This is because C has a simple linear interpretation of an array. Use the ideas found in this code to write two-dimensional routines, create_matrix, and add_matrix. These are analogous to the functions written in exercise 17.

19. Anonymous unions must be used carefully, as they are machine-dependent. Let us use them to check on conversion between the types int and float. Fill in the *Prints* column in the following table.

Declarations and assignments

```
//external to main
static union {
   int    j;
   float y;
};
//in main
int    i = 1024;
float x = 1.0;
```

Expression	Output expression	Prints
j = i	cout << j	1024
j = i	cout << y	
y = x	cout << j	
y = 2 * x	cout << y	

CHAPTER 3
Classes

This chapter introduces the reader to struct and class. The original name given by Stroustrup to his language was "C with classes." A class is an extension of the idea of struct found in traditional C. It is a way of implementing a data type and associated functions and operators. User-defined data types, such as stack, complex numbers, and card decks, are examples of ADT implementation. Each of these types is coded in C++ and used in a major example.

We will explain here the new concept of class by first reviewing how traditional C structures work. In C++, structures may have member functions. Structures also can have parts of their description private.

Both of these extensions will be described. These extensions lead naturally to the `class` concept that, in effect, is a `struct` with a default visibility of `private`.

Allowing private and public visibility for members gives the programmer control over what parts of the data structure are modifiable. The private parts are hidden from client code while the public parts are available. It is possible to change the hidden representation but not change the public access or functionality. If done properly, client code need not change when the hidden representation is modified. A large part of the OOP design process involves thinking up the appropriate ADTs for a problem. Good ADTs not only model key features of the problem but are frequently reusable in other code.

3.1. The Aggregate Type `struct`

The structure type allows the programmer to aggregate components into a single, named variable. A structure has components, called *members*, that are individually named. Since the members of a structure can be of various types, the programmer can create aggregates that are suitable for describing complicated data.

As a simple example, let us define a structure that will describe a playing card. The spots on a card that represent its numeric value are called *pips*. A playing card, such as the three of spades, has a pip value, 3, and a suit value, spades. As in Chapter 2, we can declare the structure type

```
enum suit {clubs, diamonds, hearts, spades};

struct card {
   suit   s;
   int    pips;
};
```

In traditional C, the declaration of `card` would be illegal. It would have to be

```
struct card {
   enum suit   s;
   int         pips;
};
```

As we described in Chapter 2, in C++, the tag names are types. Our examples will use this C++ innovation. In this declaration, struct is a keyword, card is the structure tag name, and the variables pips and suit are members of the structure. The variable pips will take values from 1 to 13, representing ace to king.

This declaration creates the derived data type struct card, or in C++ the type card. The declaration can be thought of as a template; it creates the type, but no storage is allocated. The declaration

```
card    c1, c2;
```

allocates storage for the identifiers c1 and c2, which are of type card. To access the members of c1 and c2, we use the structure member operator " . ". Suppose we want to assign to c1 the values representing the five of diamonds and to c2 the values representing the queen of spades. To do this we can write

```
c1.pips = 5;
c1.suit - diamonds;
c2.pips = 12;
c2.suit = spades;
```

A construct of the form

structure_variable . member_name

is used as a variable in the same way a simple variable or an element of an array is used. The member name must be unique within the specified structure. Since the member must always be prefaced or accessed through a unique structure variable identifier, there is no confusion between two members having the same name in different structures. An example is

```
struct fruit {
    char    name[15];
    int     calories;
};

struct vegetable {
    char    name[15];
    int     calories;
};

fruit       a;      //struct fruit    a; in traditional C
vegetable   b;      //struct vegetable b; in traditional C
```

Having made these declarations, we can access a.calories and b.calories without ambiguity.

3.2. Structure Pointer Operator

We have already seen the use of the member operator " . " in accessing members. In this section we introduce the structure pointer operator ->.

C provides the structure pointer operator -> to access the members of a structure via a pointer. This operator is typed on the keyboard as a minus sign followed by a greater than sign. If a pointer variable is assigned the address of a structure, then a member of the structure can be accessed by a construct of the form

pointer_to_structure -> *member_name*

An equivalent construct is given by

(**pointer_to_structure*). *member_name*

The operators -> and " . ", along with () and [], have the highest precedence, and they associate *left to right*. In complicated situations the two accessing modes can be combined. The following table illustrates their use in a straightforward manner.

Declarations and assignments		

`card cd, *p = &cd;`
`card deck[52];`
 	
`cd.pips = 5;`
`cd. suit = spades;`
`deck[0] = cd;`		

Expression	Equivalent expression	Value
`cd.pips`	`p -> pips`	5
`cd.suit`	`p -> suit`	spades
`deck[0].pips`	`deck -> pips`	5
`(*p).suit`	`p -> suit`	spades

3.3. An Example: Stack

The stack is one of the most useful standard data structures. A stack is
a data structure that allows insertion and deletion of data to occur only
at a single restricted element, the top of the stack. This is the last-in-
first-out discipline (LIFO). Conceptually, it behaves like a pile of trays
that pops up or is pushed down when trays are removed or added. Typically, a stack allows as operations *push*, *pop*, *top*, *empty*, and *full*. The
push operator places a value on the stack. The pop operator retrieves
and deletes a value off the stack. The top operator returns the top value
from the stack. The empty operator tests if the stack is empty. The full
operator tests if the stack is full. The stack is a typical ADT.

We wish to implement a stack as a C++ data type using struct
in its traditional form. An implementation choice will be to use a fixed-
length char array to store the contents of the stack. The top of the stack
will be an integer-valued member named top. The various stack operations will be implemented as functions, each of whose argument lists
includes a pointer to stack parameter. This will avoid copying a poten-
tially large stack to perform a simple operation.

```
//A traditional C implementation of type stack.

const int max_len = 1000;
enum boolean {false, true};

struct stack {
    char s[max_len];
    int  top;
};

void reset(stack* stk)
{
    stk -> top = 0;
}

void push(char c, stack* stk)
{
    stk -> top++;
    stk -> s[stk -> top] = c;
}
```

```
char pop(stack* stk)
{
   return (stk -> s[stk -> top--]);
}

char top(stack* stk)
{
   return (stk -> s[stk -> top]);
}

boolean empty(stack* stk)
{
   return (stk -> top == 0);
}

boolean full(stack* stk)
{
   return (stk -> top == max_len - 1);
}
```

■ DISSECTION OF THE *stack* FUNCTIONS

```
const int max_len = 1000;
enum boolean {false, true};

struct stack {
   char s[max_len];
   int  top;
};
```

- We declare a new type boolean. In C++ the tag name of an enum type is a new type. The constant false is initialized to 0 and the constant true is initialized to 1. The struct declaration creates the new type stack. It has two members, the array member s and the int member top.

```
void reset(stack* stk)
{
   stk -> top = 0;
}
```

- This function is used for initialization. The member top is assigned the value 0. The stack starts out as empty. The particular stack that this works on is an argument passed in aș an address.

```
void push(char c, stack* stk)
{
    stk -> top++;
    stk -> s[stk -> top] = c;
}

char pop(stack* stk)
{
    return (stk -> s[stk -> top--]);
}
```

- The operation *push* is implemented as a function of two arguments. The member top is incremented. The value of c is shoved onto the top of the stack. This function assumes that the stack is not full. The operation *pop* is implemented in a like fashion. It assumes the stack is not empty. The value of the top of the stack is returned, and the member top is decremented.

```
boolean empty(stack* stk)
{
    return (stk -> top == 0);
}

boolean full(stack* stk)
{
    return (stk -> top == max_len - 1);
}
```

- These functions return an enumerated type boolean value. Each tests the stack member top for an appropriate condition. In all functions the stack argument is passed in as address and the structure pointer operator -> is used to access members.

Given that these declarations reside in the file stack.h, we can test these operations with the following program, which enters the characters of a string onto a stack and pops them, printing each character out in reverse order:

```
//Test of stack implementation by reversing a string.

#include <stream.h>
#include "stack.h"        //stack implementation imported

main()
{
    stack       s;
    static char str[40] = {"My name is Betty Dolsberry!"};
    int         i = 0;

    cout << str << "\n";        //print the string
    reset(&s);
    while (str[i])              //push onto stack
        if (!full(&s))
            push(str[i++], &s);
    while (!empty(&s))          //print the reverse
        cout << form("%c", pop(&s));
    cout << "\n";
}
```

The output from this test program is

```
My name is Betty Dolsberry!
!yrrebsloD ytteB si eman yM
```

Note that one of the actual arguments to each function is &s, the address of the stack variable declared in main. This argument is given because each function expects an address of a stack variable. The output function form is analogous to printf in *stdio.h*. It produces formatted output for a list of arguments (see Section 7.2).

3.4. Member Functions

The concept of struct is augmented in C++ to allow functions to be members. The function declaration is included in the structure declaration and is invoked by using access methods for structure members. The idea is that the functionality required by the struct data type should be directly included in the struct declaration. This construct improves the encapsulation of the ADT stack operations by packaging it directly with its data representation.

Let us rewrite our stack example by declaring as member functions, the various functions associated with the stack.

```
struct stack {
    //data representation

    char  s[max_len];
    int   top;

    //operations represented as member functions

    void    reset() { top = 0; }
    void    push(char c) { top++; s[top] = c; }
    char    pop() { return (s[top--]); }
    char    top_of() { return (s[top]); }
    boolean empty() { return (top == 0); }
    boolean full() { return (top == max_len - 1); }
};
```

The member functions are written much as other functions. One difference is that they can use the data member names as is. Thus the member functions in stack use top and s in an unqualified manner. When invoked on a particular object of type stack, they act on the specified member in that object.

The following example illustrates these ideas. If two stack variables

```
stack data, operands;
```

are declared, then

```
data.reset();
operands.reset();
```

invoke the member function reset, which has the effect of setting both data.top and operands.top to 0. If a pointer to stack

```
stack* ptr_operands = &operands;
```

is declared, then

```
ptr_operands -> push('A');
```

invokes the member function push, which has the effect of incrementing operands.top and setting operands.s[top] to 'A'. One last observation: The member function top_of had its name changed from the previous implementation because of a naming conflict.

Member functions that are defined within the struct are implicitly inline. As a rule, only short, heavily used member functions should be defined within the struct, as is the case for the example just given. To define a member function outside the struct, the scope resolution operator is used. Let us illustrate this by changing the definition of push to its corresponding function prototype within the struct stack. We write it out fully using the scope resolution operator. In this case the function is not implicitly inline.

```
struct stack {
    //data representation

    char s[max_len];
    int  top;

    //operations represented as member functions

    void reset() { top = 0; } //definition, implicitly inline
    void push(char c);        //function prototype
    . . .
};

    void stack::push(char c)  //definition, not inline
    {
        top++;
        s[top] = c;
    }
```

The scope resolution operator allows member functions from the different struct types to have the same names. In this case, which member function is invoked will depend on the type of object it acts upon. Member functions within the same struct can be overloaded. Consider adding to the data type stack a pop operation that has an integer parameter that is the number of times the stack should be popped. It could be added as the following function prototype within the struct:

```
char pop(int n);                    //within stack
char stack::pop(int n)
{
    while(n-- > 1)
        top--;
    return (s[top--]);
}
```

The definition that is invoked depends on the actual arguments to pop.

```
data.pop();                         //invokes standard pop
data.pop(5);                        //invokes iterated pop
```

3.5. Visibility private and public

The concept of struct is augmented in C++ to allow structures to have public and private members. Inside a struct, the use of the keyword private followed by a colon restricts the scope of the members that follow this construct. The private members can be used by only a few categories of functions, whose privileges include access to these members. These functions include the member functions of the struct. Other categories of functions having access will be discussed later.

We modify our example of stack to hide its data representation.

```
struct stack {
private:
    char  s[max_len];
    int   top;
public:
    void    reset() { top = 0; }
    void    push(char c) { top++; s[top] = c; }
    char    pop() { return (s[top--]); }
    char    top_of() { return (s[top]); }
    boolean empty() { return (top == 0); }
    boolean full() { return (top == max_len - 1); }
};
```

We now rewrite `main` from Section 3.3 to test the same operations.

```
main()
{
    stack       s;
    static char str[40] = {"My name is Don Knuth!"};
    int         i = 0;

    cout << str << "\n";
    s.reset();                      //s.top = 0; would be illegal
    while (str[i])
        if (!s.full())
            s.push(str[i++]);
    while (!s.empty())          //print the reverse
        cout << form("%c", s.pop());
    cout << "\n";
}
```

The output from this version of the test program is

```
My name is Don Knuth!
!htunK noD si eman yM
```

As the comment in `main` states, access to the hidden variable `top` is controlled. It can be changed by the member function `reset` but cannot be accessed directly. Also notice how the variable `s` is passed to each member function using the structure member operator form.

The `struct stack` has a private part that contains its data description and a public part that contains member functions to implement stack operations. It is useful to think of the private part as restricted to the implementor's use, and the public part to be an interface specification that clients may use. At a later time, the implementor could change the private part without affecting the correctness of a client's use of the stack type.

Hiding data is an important component of OOP. It allows for more easily debugged and maintained code, because errors and modifications are localized. Client programs need only be aware of the type's interface specification.

3.6. Classes

Classes in C++ are introduced by the keyword `class`. They are a form
of `struct` whose default privacy specification is `private`. Thus `struct`
and `class` can be used interchangeably with the appropriate privacy
specification.

Many scientific computations require complex numbers. Let us
write an ADT for complex numbers.

```
struct complex {
private:
    double real, imag;
public:
    void    assign(double r, double i);
    void    print() { cout << real << " + " << imag << "i"; }
};

void complex::assign(double r, double i = 0.0)
{
    real - r;
    imag = i;
}
```

Here is its equivalent `class` representation.

```
class complex {
    double real, imag;
public:
    void    assign(double r, double i);
    void    print() { cout << real << " + " << imag << "i "; }
};

void complex::assign(double r, double i = 0.0)
{
    real = r;
    imag = i;
}
```

Notice the only difference is in the use of the keywords `public` and `private`. Also possible would have been

```
class complex {
private:          //one style is to make this explicit
   double real, imag;
public:
   void   assign(double r, double i);
   void   print() { cout << real << " + " << imag << "i "; }
};
```

It will be our style to prefer `class` to `struct` unless all members are to be treated as `public`.

3.7. `static` **Member**

Data members can be declared with the storage class modifier `static`. They cannot be declared `auto`, `register`, or `extern`. A data member that is declared `static` is shared by all variables of that class and is stored uniquely in one place. Because of this it can be accessed in the form

class name :: *identifier*

as well as normal member access. This is a further use of the scope resolution operator (see Section 2.5). A `static` member of a global class must be explicitly declared and defined in file scope. An example is

```
enum boolean {false, true};

class str {
   char              s[100];
public:
   static boolean  read_only;
   void            print();
   void            assign(char*);
      . . .
};

boolean str::read_only = false;  //file scope initialization
```

In our example this could be used to decide whether an object of type str could be changed in value. So,

```
str s1, s2, s3, s4;
if (!str::read_only)
    s1.assign("Buzz Dolsberry");
```

is a means of conveniently maintaining a value common to the entire class.

3.8. Nested Classes

Classes can be nested. The rules for nesting classes are in transition. C++ release 2.0 rules state that the inner class is not inside the scope of the outer class, but rather has the same scope as the outer class. Since this can lead to confusion, nesting class declarations is normally poor style.

The following incorrectly nested classes illustrate these points:

```
char c;                    //external scope

class X {                  //outer class declaration
    char c;
    class Y {              //inner class declaration
        char d;
        void foo(char e) { c - e; }
    };
    char goo(X* q) { return (q -> d); }   //illegal
};
```

In class Y the member function foo, when using c, means the external scope c. It is as if class Y were declared at the same level and inside the same block or file scope as class X. In class X the member function goo, when using d, is attempting to access a private member of class Y.

3.9. An Example: Flushing

We wish to estimate the probability of being dealt a flush. A flush occurs when at least five cards are of the same suit. We will simulate shuffling cards by using a random number generator to shuffle the deck. This is a form of *Monte Carlo* calculation. The program will be written using classes to represent the needed data types and functionality.

```
//A poker calculation on flushing

#include  <stream.h>

int    random(void);              //random number generator
void   srandom(unsigned int seed);  //if unavailable use
unsigned   seed;                  //rand and srand

enum suit {clubs, diamonds, hearts, spades};

class pips {
    int  p;
public:
    void assign(int n) { p = n % 13 + 1; }
    int  getpip() { return (p); }
    void print();
};

class card {
    int  cd;                          //a cd is from 0 to 51
public:
    suit s;
    pips p;
    void assign(int n) { cd = n; s = n / 13; p.assign(n); }
    void pr_card();
};

class deck {
    card d[52];
public:
    void init_deck();
    void shuffle();
    void deal(int, int, card*);
    void pr_deck();
};
```

We used an enumerated type suit to represent card suits. The enumerated constants are mapped into the integers 0, 1, 2, and 3. So clubs is the integer value 0 and spades is the integer value 3. Each level of declaration hides the complexity of the previous level. Notice also that we can plan to code the functions later on. For example, we will not use the print routines in this example; they can be added as needed.

A most interesting function is the implicitly inline function

```
void assign(int n) { cd = n;  s = n / 13;  p.assign(n);  }
```

which uses the function `void pips::assign(int n);`. We could have used the notation

```
p.pips::assign(n)
```

to show clearly that this function is from the class `pips`, but this is unnecessary. The function maps an integer whose value is between 0 and 51 into a unique pair of `suit` and `pips` values. The value 0 becomes the ace of clubs and the value 51 becomes the king of spades.

The other member functions are not inline and are defined at a later point with the use of the scope resolution operator.

```
void   deck::init_deck()
{
    for (int i = 0;  i < 52;  ++i)
        d[i].assign(i);
}

void   deck::shuffle()
{
    for (int i = 0;  i < 52;  ++i) {
        int k = random() % 52;
        card t = d[i]; d[i] = d[k]; d[k] = t;  //swap two cards
    }
}

void deck::deal(int n,  int pos,  card* hand)
{
    for (int i = pos;  i < pos + n;  ++i)
        hand[i - pos] = d[i];
}
```

The `init_deck` function calls `card::assign` to map the integers into card values. The `shuffle` function uses the library-supplied pseudorandom number generator `random` to exchange two cards for every deck position. Tests show that this gives a reasonable approximation to good shuffling. The `deal` function takes cards in sequence from the deck and arranges them into hands.

It now remains to use these functions to estimate a probability that a flush occurs when poker hands are dealt. The operator can choose to deal out between five and nine cards per hand.

```
main()
{
    card one_hand[9];                       //max hand is 9 cards
    deck dk;
    int   i, j, k, fcnt = 0, sval[4];
    int   ndeal, nc, nhand;

    do {
        cout << "\nEnter no. of cards in each hand (5-9): ";
        cin  >> nc;
    } while (nc < 5 || nc > 9);
    nhand = 52 / nc;

    cout << "\nEnter no. of hands to deal and a random seed: ";
    cin  >> ndeal >> seed;

    srandom(seed);
    dk.init_deck();
    for (k = 0; k < ndeal; k += nhand) {
        if ((nhand + k) > ndeal)
            nhand = ndeal - k;
        dk.shuffle();
        for (i = 0; i < nc * nhand; i += nc) {
            for (j = 0; j < 4; ++j)          //init suit counts to 0
                sval[j] = 0;
            dk.deal(nc, i, one_hand);        //deal next hand
            for (j = 0; j < nc; ++j)
                sval[one_hand[j].s] ++ ;     //increment suit count
            for (j = 0; j < 4; ++j)
                if (sval[j] >= 5)            //5 or more is flush
                    fcnt++;
        }
    }
    cout << "\n\nIn " << ndeal << " ";
    cout << nc << "-card hands there were ";
    cout << fcnt << " flushes\n    ";
}
```

■ DISSECTION OF THE *flush* PROGRAM

```
card one_hand[9];              //max hand is 9 cards
deck dk;
int   i, j, k, fcnt = 0, sval[4];
int   ndeal, nc, nhand;
```

- These are variables allocated upon block entry when `main` is executed. The variable `one_hand` is an array of nine elements, the maximum hand size allowed. It will be used to store dealt-out hands from the deck. The variable `dk` represents our deck and is automatically allocated. All its data members are created, though some are hidden. The number of cards dealt to each hand is stored as the variable `nc`, and the number of hands to be dealt is kept in the variable `ndeal`. The variable `fcnt` will count the number of flushes. The array `sval` is used to store the number of cards found in the hand of a particular suit value.

```
do {
    cout << "\nEnter no. of cards in each hand (5-9): ";
    cin  >> nc;
} while (nc < 5 || nc > 9);
nhand = 52 / nc;

cout << "\nEnter no. of hands to deal and a random seed: ";
cin  >> ndeal >> seed;

srandom(seed);
```

- We prompt for the number of cards to deal to each hand. The operator must respond with a number between 5 and 9 in order to proceed. The number of hands that can be dealt with the deck is computed and put into the variable `nhand`. We prompt for the number of deals and the initial seed. Different values for `seed` give different random number sequences. Using the same choice leads to the same result.

```
dk.init_deck();
for (k = 0; k < ndeal; k += nhand) {
   if ((nhand + k) > ndeal)
      nhand = ndeal - k;
   dk.shuffle();
```

- The deck variable dk is initialized, and each time through the main loop the deck is reshuffled. The variable dk is implicitly an argument to the called member functions init_deck and shuffle. The test to check whether the value of ndeal has been exceeded ensures that the total number of hands dealt will not exceed the request if the total number of hands is not an even multiple of the number of hands per shuffle.

```
for (i = 0; i < nc * nhand; i += nc) {
   for (j = 0; j < 4; ++j)                   //init suit counts to 0
      sval[j] = 0;
   dk.deal(nc, i, one_hand);                 //deal next hand
   for (j = 0; j > nc; ++j)
      sval[one_hand[j].s] ++ ;               //increment suit count
   for (j = 0; j < 4; ++j)
      if (sval[j] >= 5)                      //5 or more is flush
         fcnt++;
}
```

- The array sval stores the number of cards of each suit and is initialized to zero for each hand. The function deck::deal deals a card hand into the array one_hand. The expression one_hand[j].s is the suit value of a particular card, for example, 0 if the card were a club. This then is the index of the array sval that counts suits. The variable fcnt winds up with the number of flushes dealt over all these trials. Since the number of trials equals ndeal, the expectation of a flush is fcnt/ndeal.

3.10. Summary

1. The original name given by Stroustrup to his language was "C with classes." A `class` is an extension of the idea of `struct` in traditional C. It is a way of implementing a data type and associated functions and operators. It also is the mechanism in C++ for implementing ADTs, such as complex numbers and stacks.

2. The structure type allows the programmer to aggregate components into a single, named variable. A structure has components, called *members,* that are individually named. Critical to processing structures is the accessing of their members. This is done with either the member operator " . " or the structure pointer operator ->. These operators, along with () and [], have the highest precedence.

3. The concept of `struct` is augmented in C++ to allow functions to be members. The function declaration is included in the structure declaration and is invoked by using access methods for structure members. The idea is that the functionality required by the `struct` data type should be directly included in the `struct` declaration.

4. Member functions that are defined within the `struct` are implicitly inline. As a rule only short, heavily used member functions should be defined within the `struct`. To define a member function outside the `struct`, the scope resolution operator is used.

5. The scope resolution operator allows member functions from the different `struct` types to have the same names. In this case, which member function is invoked will depend on the type of object it acts upon. Member functions within the same `struct` can be overloaded.

6. The concept of `struct` is augmented in C++ to allow functions to have `public` and `private` members. This provides *data hiding.* Inside a `struct`, the use of the keyword `private` followed by a colon restricts the scope of the members that follow this construct. The `private` members can be used by only a few categories of functions, whose privileges include access to these members. These functions include the member functions of the `struct`.

7. Classes in C++ are introduced by the keyword `class`. They are a form of `struct` whose default privacy specification is `private`. Thus `struct` and `class` can be used interchangeably with the appropriate privacy specification.

8. Data members can be declared with the storage class modifier `static`. A data member that is declared `static` is shared by all variables of that class and is stored uniquely in one place. Because of this it can be accessed in the form

   class name :: *identifier*

9. Classes can be nested. The inner class is not inside the scope of the outer class, but rather has the same scope as the outer class. This is not a recommended practice.

3.11. Exercises

1. Design a traditional C structure to store a dairy product's name, portion weight, calories, protein, fat, and carbohydrates. Twenty-five grams of American cheese has 375 calories, 5 grams of protein, 8 grams of fat, and 0 grams of carbohydrates. Show how to assign these values to the member variables of your structure. Write a function that, given a variable of type `struct dairy` and a given weight in grams (portion size), returns the number of calories for that weight.

2. Use the `struct card` defined in Section 3.1 and write a hand-sorting routine. In card games most players keep their cards sorted by pip value. The routine will place aces first, kings next, and so forth, down to twos. A hand will be five cards.

3. The following declarations do not compile correctly. Explain what is wrong.

```
struct brother {
    char          name[20];
    int           age;
    struct sister sib;
} a;

struct sister {
    char           name[20];
    int            age;
    struct brother sib;
} a;
```

4. In this exercise use the `struct stack` defined in Section 3.3. Write the function

```
void reverse(char s1[], char s2[]);
```

The strings s1 and s2 must be the same size. String s2 should become a reversed copy of string s1. Internal to reverse use a stack to perform the reversal.

5. Rewrite the functions push and pop in Section 3.3 to test that push is not acting on a full stack and pop is not acting on an empty stack. If either condition is detected, print an error message using cerr and use exit(1) to abort the program.

6. Write reverse (see exercise 4) as a member function for type stack in Section 3.4. Test it by printing normally and reversed the string

```
Gottfried Leibniz wrote Toward a Universal Characteristic
```

7. For the stack type in Section 3.4 write as member functions

```
//push n chars from s1[1] onto the stack
void pushm(int n, char s1[]);

//pop n chars from stack into char string
void popm(int n, char s1[]);
```

Hint: Be sure to output a terminator character into the string before outputting it.

8. What is the difference in meaning between the structure

```
struct a {
    int i, j, k;
};
```

and the class

```
class a {
    int i, j, k;
};
```

Explain why the class declaration is not useful. How can you use the keyword `public` to change the class declaration into a declaration equivalent to struct a?

9. We wish to define the `class deque` to implement a double-ended queue. A double-ended queue allows push and pop at both ends.

```
class deque {
    char s[max_len];
    int  bottom, top;
public:
    void reset() { top = bottom = max_len / 2; top--; }
    . . .
};
```

Declare and implement `push_t`, `pop_t`, `push_b`, `pop_b`, `out_stack`, `top_of`, `bottom_of`, `empty`, and `full`. The function `push_t` stands for *push on top*. The function `push_b` stands for *push on bottom*. The `out_stack` function should output the stack from its bottom to its top. The `pop_t` and `pop_b` functions correspond to *pop from top* and *pop from bottom*. An empty stack is denoted by having the top fall below the bottom. Test each function.

10. Extend the data type `deque` by adding a member function `relocate`. If the `deque` is full, then `relocate` is called and the contents of the `deque` are moved to balance empty storage around the center `max_len / 2` of array s. Its function declaration header is

```
//returns true if it succeeds, false if it fails
boolean deque::relocate()
```

11. Write a swap function that swaps the contents of two strings. If you pushed a string of characters onto a stack and popped them into a second string, they would come out reversed. In a swap of two strings we want the original ordering. Use a `deque` to swap two strings. The strings will be stored in two character arrays of the same length, but the strings themselves may be of differing lengths. The function prototype is

```
void swap(char s1[], char s2[]);
```

12. Write the following member functions:

```
void pips::print();
void card::pr_card();
void deck::pr_deck();
```

and add them to the *flush* program found in Section 3.9. Let pr_deck use pr_card and pr_card use print. Print the deck after it is initialized.

13. Write a function pr_hand that prints out card hands. Add it to the *flush* program and use it to print out each flush.

14. In Section 3.9 main detects flushes. Write a function

```
boolean isflush(card hand[], int nc);
```

that returns true if a hand is a flush.

15. Write a function

```
boolean isstraight(card hand[], nc);
```

that returns true if a hand is a straight. A straight is five cards that have sequential pips value. The lowest straight is ace, two, three, four, five and the highest straight is ten, jack, queen, king, ace. Run experiments to estimate the probability that dealt-out cards will be a straight and compare the results of 5-card hands with results of 7-card hands.

Hint: You may want to set up an array of 15 integers to correspond to counters for each pips value. Be sure that a pip value of 1 (corresponding to aces) is also counted as the high card corresponding to a pip value of 14.

16. Use the previous exercises to determine the probability that a poker hand will be a straight flush. This is a hand that is both a straight and flush. It is the hardest poker hand to get and has the highest

value. Note that in a hand of more than five cards, it is not sufficient to merely check for the presence of both a straight and a flush to determine that the hand is a straight flush.

17. Change the `suit` declaration from an enumerated type to a class as follows:

```
enum {clubs, diamonds, hearts, spades};

class suit {
    enum {clubs, diamonds, hearts, spades} s;
public:
    void assign(int n) { s = n / 13; }
    int  getsuit() { return (s); }
    void print();
};
```

We use an anonymous `enum` to define the four integer constants used for suit values. We add the member function `getsuit` to access the hidden integer value of a `suit` variable. Now recode all references to suit throughout the program.

CHAPTER 4
Constructors and Destructors

A constructor is a member function whose name is the same as the class name. It *constructs* values of the class type. This process involves initializing of data members and, frequently, allocating free store using new. A destructor is a member function whose name is the class name preceded by the character ~. Its usual purpose is to *destroy* values of the class type, typically by using delete.

Constructors are the more complicated of these two specially named member functions. They may be overloaded and can take arguments, neither of which is possible for destructors. Constructors are invoked when their associated type is used in a declaration. They are also invoked when call-by-value is used to pass a value to a function. Constructors and destructors do not have return types nor can they use `return` statements. Destructors are implicitly invoked when an object of its class must be destroyed, typically upon block exit or function exit.

4.1. Classes with Constructors

The simplest use of a constructor is for initialization. We will develop some examples in this and later sections that will use constructors to initialize the values of the data members of the class. Not all classes can have constructors. A variable of a class having a constructor cannot be a member of a `union`. A class with a static member cannot have a constructor.

Our first example is an implementation of a data type `mod_int` to store numbers that are computed with a modulus.

```
// Modulo numbers and constructor initialization

#include <stream.h>

const int modulus = 60;
class mod_int {
    int   v;
public:
    mod_int(int i) { v = i % modulus; }
    void assign(int i) { v = i % modulus; }
    void print() { cout << v << "\t"; }
};
```

The integer v will be restricted in value to 0, 1, 2, . . . `modulus` − 1. It is the programmer's responsibility to enforce this restriction by having all member functions guarantee this behavior. The member function `mod_int` is a constructor. It does not have a return type. Some examples of declarations using this type are:

```
mod_int   a(0);    // a.v = 0;
mod_int   b(61);   // b.v = 1;
```

but not

```
mod_int   a;        // no parameter list
```

Using this type, we can write code to convert seconds into minutes and seconds as follows.

```
main()
{
    int      seconds = 400;
    mod_int z(seconds);

    cout << seconds << " seconds equals "
         << seconds / 60 << " minutes ";
    z.print();
    cout << " seconds\n";
}
```

It is often convenient to overload the constructor with several function declarations. In our example, it could be desirable to have the default value of v be 0. By adding the constructor

```
mod_int() { v = 0; }
```

as a member function of mod_int, it is possible to have the following declarations:

```
mod_int s1, s2;   // both initialize the private member v to 0
mod_int d[5];     // arrays are properly initialized
```

In both of these declarations the empty parameter list constructor is invoked. Classes with constructors that have a constructor with a void argument list can be the base type of an array declaration. A class with constructors that always require parameters cannot be the base type of an array declaration. In C++ terminology such declarations are also called *vector* declarations.

A constructor can also be used to allocate space from free store. We will modify the stack type from Chapter 3 to have its maximum length be initialized by a constructor.

```
//stack implementation with constructor
class stack {
    //the hidden representation for the ADT stack
    char* s;            //changed from
    int    max_len;     //s[max_len]
    int    top;
public:
    //the public interface for the ADT stack
    stack(int size) { s = new char[size];
                        max_len = size; top = 0; }
    void    reset() { top = 0; }
    void    push(char c) { top++; s[top] = c; }
    char    pop() { return (s[top--]); }
    char    top_of() { return (s[top]); }
    boolean empty() { return (top == 0); }
    boolean full() { return (top == max_len - 1); }
};
```

An example of a stack declaration invoking this constructor is

```
stack data(1000);      // allocate 1000 element char stack
```

Two alternate constructors would be an empty parameter constructor that would allocate a specific length stack, and a two-parameter constructor whose second parameter is a string used to initialize the stack. They could be written as follows:

```
stack::stack(void)
{
    s = new char[100];
    max_len = 100;
    top = 0;
}

stack::stack(int size, char str[])
{
    s = new char[size];
    max_len = size;
    for ( int i = 0; i < max_len && str[i] != 0; ++i)
        s[i] = str[i];
    top = i;
}
```

The corresponding function prototypes would be included as members of the class stack.

4.2. Classes with Destructors

Destructors are member functions whose name is the same as the class name preceded by a tilde. They cannot be explicitly called, and usually are associated with classes where data members are dynamically allocated from free store. A variable of a class having a destructor cannot be a member of a union.

Let us augment our stack example with a destructor.

```
//stack implementation with constructors and destructor
class stack {
    char* s;
    int    max_len;
    int    top;
public:
    stack(int size) { s = new char[size];
                        max_len = size; top = 0; }
    stack(void);
    stack(int size, char str[]);
    ~stack(void) { delete s; }     //destructor
    . . .
};
```

The external interface of this class remains the same. In other words, all the public member functions perform in exactly the same manner as before. The difference is that the destructor will be implicitly invoked upon block and function exit to clean up storage that is no longer accessible. This is good programming practice and allows programs to execute with less available memory.

4.3. An Example: Dynamically Allocated Strings

A string type is lacking in traditional C. Strings in C are represented as pointer to char and manipulated accordingly. In this representation the end-of-string is denoted by \0. This convention has an important drawback in that many basic string manipulations are proportional to string length. When the string length is known, the efficiency of operations on strings can be significantly improved.

We will develop a useful string ADT in this section that stores its length privately. We want our type to be dynamically allocated, and able to represent arbitrary length strings. A variety of constructors will be coded to initialize and allocate strings, and a set of operations on strings will be coded as member functions. The implementation will use the *string.h* library functions to manipulate the underlying pointer representation of strings.

```
//An implementation of dynamically allocated strings.
#include <string.h>
#include <stream.h>

class string {
   char* s;
   int   len;
public:
   string() { s = new char[81]; len = 80; }
   string(int n) { s = new char[n + 1]; len = n; }
   string(char* p) { len = strlen(p);
                     s = new char[len + 1]; strcpy(s, p); }
   string(string& str);
   ~string() { delete s; }
   void assign(char* str) { strcpy(s, str);
                            len = strlen(str); }
   void print() { cout << s << "\n"; }
   void concat(string& a, string& b);
};

string::string(string& str)
{
   len = str.len;
   s = new char[len + 1];
   strcpy(s, str.s);
}

void string::concat(string& a, string& b)
{
   len = a.len + b.len;
   delete s;
   s = new char[len + 1];
   strcpy(s, a.s);
   strcat(s, b.s);
}
```

This type allows you to declare strings, assign a character array to a string, print a string, and concatenate two strings. The hidden representation is pointer to `char` and has a variable `len` in which to store the current string length. The constructors all allocate dynamically from free store.

■ DISSECTION OF THE *string* CLASS

```
string() { s = new char[81]; len = 80; }
string(int n) { s = new char[n + 1]; len = n; }
string(char* p) { len = strlen(p);
                    s = new char[len + 1]; strcpy(s, p); }
string(string& str);
```

- There are four overloaded constructors. The first is the empty parameter default, which also allows us to declare an array of strings. The second has an `int` parameter that is used to initialize the string length variable `len` and to retrieve that much store using `new`. The third constructor has a pointer to `char` argument that can be used to transform the traditional C representation of strings to our `class` type. It uses two library functions: `strlen` and `strcpy`. We allocate one additional character to store the end-of-string character `\0`, although this character is not counted by `strlen`. The fourth constructor will be explained below.

```
~string() { delete s; }
```

- The destructor automatically returns memory allocated to strings back to free store for reuse. The operator `delete` knows the amount of memory associated with the pointer `s` as base address.

```
void assign(char* str) { strcpy(s, str);
                        len = strlen(str); }
void print() { cout << s << "\n"; }
```

- These two inline member functions provide an assignment and print operation, respectively. The assignment takes the traditional C representation pointer to `char` and uses `strcpy` to copy this to the private member variable `s`.

```
string::string(string& str)
{
   len = str.len;
   s = new char[len + 1];
   strcpy(s, str.s);
}
```

- This form of constructor is used to perform copying of one string value into another when:

1. A string is initialized by another string

2. A string is passed as an argument in a function

3. A string is returned as the value of a function

In older C++ systems, if this constructor is not present, then these operations are bitwise copy. In newer systems, the default is member-by-member assignment of value.

```
void string::concat(string& a, string& b)
{
    len = a.len + b.len;
    delete s;
    s = new char[len + 1];
    strcpy(s, a.s);
    strcat(s, b.s);
}
```

- This is a form of string concatenation. The two string arguments are not modified. The implicit argument, whose hidden member variables are s and len, is modified to represent the string a followed by the string b. Note that in this member function the use of len, a.len, and b.len is possible. Member functions have access not only to the private members of the implicit argument, but also to the private representation of any of the arguments.

The following code tests this type by concatenating several strings:

```
main()
{
    char*    str = "The wheel that squeaks the loudest\n";
    string   a(str), b, author("Josh Billings\n"), both, quote;

    b.assign("Is the one that gets the grease\n");
    both.concat(a, b);
    quote.concat(both, author);
    quote.print();
}
```

The printout from this program is:

```
The wheel that squeaks the loudest
Is the one that gets the grease
Josh Billings
```

We deliberately used a variety of declarations to show how different constructors would be called. The string variables b, both, and quote all use the empty argument list constructor. The declaration for author uses the constructor whose argument type is char*, which is the type of a literal C string. The concatenation takes place in two steps. First, strings a and b are concatenated into both. Next, strings both and author are concatenated into quote. It is important to understand that both is an argument to concat and is used internally wherever the unqualified member names are written.

4.4. A Class vect

It is useful to think of a one-dimensional array as a form of *vector* type. However, the traditional C array is error prone. A common mistake is to access elements that are *out of bounds*. C++ allows us to control this problem by defining an analogous array type in which bounds can be tested.

```
//Implementation of a safe array type vect
#include <stream.h>

class vect {
    int* p;
    int  size;
public:
    int  ub;                   //upper bound = size - 1
    vect() { size = 10; p = new int[size]; ub = size - 1; }
    vect(int n);
    ~vect() { delete p; }
    int& element(int i);
};

vect::vect(int n)
{
    if (n <= 0) {
        cerr << "illegal vect size " << n << "\n";
        exit(1);
    }
    size = n;
    p = new int[size];
    ub = size - 1;
}

int& vect::element(int i)
{
    if (i < 0 || i > ub) {
        cerr << "illegal vect index " << i << "\n";
        exit(1);
    }
    return (p[i]);
}
```

The constructor vect::vect(int n) allows the user to build dynamically allocated arrays. Such arrays are much more flexible than those in traditional C, where array sizes must be constant expressions. The constructor also initializes the variable ub, whose value is the array upper bound. Access to individual elements is through the safe indexing member function `int& vect::element(int i)`. An index that is outside the expected array range 0 through `ub` will cause an error message and error exit. This safe indexing member function returns a reference to `int`, that is the address of `p[i]` and that can be used as the left operand of an assignment or *lvalue*. The technique is much used in C++ and will be an efficient mechanism for operating on complicated types.

As an example, the declarations

```
vect a(10), b(5);
```

construct an array of 10 integers and an array of 5 integers, respectively. Individual elements can be accessed by the member function `element`, which checks whether the index is out of range. The statements

```
a.element(1) = 5;
b.element(1) = a.element(1) + 7;
cout << a.element(1) - 2;
```

are all legal. In effect we have a safe dynamic array type.

Classes with constructors having an empty argument list can have a derived array type. For example

```
vect a[5];
```

is a declaration that uses the empty argument constructor to create an array a of five objects, each of which is a size 10 `vect`. The `i`th element's address in the `j`th array would be given by `a[j].element(i)`.

4.5. Members that are Class Types

In this section we will use the type `vect` as part of a new class. We wish to store multiple values for each index. For example, we may want to store the age, weight, and height of a group of individuals. We could group three arrays together inside a new class.

```
#include "vect.h"

class multi_v {
public:
    vect a, b, c;
    multi_v(int i):a(i), b(i), c(i) { }
};
```

The class has three vect members and a constructor, which has an empty body but a list of constructor calls separated by commas. These constructors are executed with the integer argument i creating the three class objects a, b, and c. In early versions of the C++ language the order of constructor invocation was unspecified. In newer versions the order is as written in the comma-separated list, followed by any default initializations.

Let us test this class by writing code to store and print a set of values for age in years, weight in pounds, and height in inches.

```
main()
{
    multi_v a_w_h(5);   //age weight and height

    for (int i = 0; i <= a_w_h.a.ub; ++i) {
        a_w_h.a.element(i) = 21 + i;
        a_w_h.b.element(i) = 135 + i;
        a_w_h.c.element(i) = 62 + i;
    }
    for (i = 0; i <= a_w_h.a.ub; ++i) {
        cout << a_w_h.a.element(i) << " years ";
        cout << a_w_h.b.element(i) << " pounds ";
        cout << a_w_h.c.element(i) << " inches\n";
    }
}
```

The declaration of a_w_h creates three vect members each of five elements. When the program is executed, the individual destructors for each vect member will be called upon block exit from main. The ordering of destructor calls in newer C++ systems is to be the reverse of the call on constructors. When executed, the above program will print:

```
21 years 135 pounds 62 inches
22 years 136 pounds 63 inches
23 years 137 pounds 64 inches
24 years 138 pounds 65 inches
25 years 139 pounds 66 inches
```

4.6. An Example: A Singly Linked List

In this section we develop a singly linked list data type. This is the prototype of many useful dynamic data structures called *self-referential* structures. These data types have pointer members that refer to objects of their own type. A linked list is like a clothes line on which the data elements hang sequentially. The head of the line is the only immediate access point, and items can readily be added to or deleted from it. The following class declaration implements such a type.

```
//A singly linked list

#include <stream.h>

struct listelem {
    char        data;
    listelem*   next;
};

class list {
    listelem*   h;                //head of list
public:
    list() { h = 0; }             //0 is the NULL pointer value
    ~list() { release(); }
    void        add(char c);      //adds to front of list
    void        del() { listelem* temp = h;
                        h = h -> next;
                        delete temp; }
    listelem* first() { return (h); }
    void        pr_list();
    void        release();
};
```

The link member next is self-referential. The variable data in this example is a simple variable, but it could be replaced by a complicated type capable of storing a range of information. The constructor initializes the head of list pointer h to the value 0, which is called the *null pointer constant*. It can be assigned to any pointer type. In linked lists it typically denotes the empty list or end-of-list value. The member function add is used to build the list structure.

```
void list::add(char c)
{
    listelem* temp = new listelem;    //create new element

    temp -> next = h;                 //link to list
    temp -> data = c;
    h = temp;                         //update head of list
}
```

A list element is allocated from free store and its data member is initialized from the single argument c. Its link member next points at the old head of list. The head pointer h is then updated to point at this element as the new first element of the list.

The inline member function del has the inverse role. It returns the first element of the list to free store. It does this by using the delete operator on the head of list pointer h. The new head of list is the value of the next member.

Much of list processing is repetitively chaining down the list until the null pointer value is found. The following two functions use this technique.

```
void list::pr_list()
{
    listelem*  temp = h;

    while (temp != 0) {              //detect end of list
        cout << form("%c -> ", temp -> data);
        temp = temp -> next;
    }
    cout << "\n###\n";
}

void list::release()  //elements are returned to free store
{
    while (h != 0)
        del();
}
```

■ DISSECTION OF THE *pr_list* AND *release* FUNCTIONS

```
void list::pr_list()
{
    listelem*  temp = h;
```

● An auxiliary pointer temp will be used to chain down the list. It is initialized to the address of the list head h. The pointer h cannot be used because its value would be lost, in effect destroying access to the list.

```
while (temp != 0) {                          //detect end of list
    cout << form("%c -> ", temp -> data);
    temp = temp -> next;
}
```

- The value 0 represents the end-of-list value. It is guaranteed to be such because the constructor list::list initialized it and the list::add function maintains it as the end-of-list pointer value. Notice that the internals of this loop could be changed to process the entire list in some other manner.

```
void list::release()    //each element is returned to free store
```

- The release function is used to return all list elements to free store. It marches down the list doing so.

```
while (h != 0)
    del();
```

- Each element of the list must be returned to free store in sequence. This is done for a single element by the member function del, which manipulates the hidden pointer h. Since we are destroying the list, it is unnecessary to preserve the original value of pointer h. This function's chief use is as the body of the destructor list::~list. We could not use a destructor written

```
list::~list()
{
    delete h;
}
```

because it only deletes the first element in the list.

We demonstrate the use of this type in the following code:

```
main()
{
    list*  p;
    {
        list      w;

        w.add('A');
        w.add('B');
        w.pr_list();
        w.del();
        w.pr_list();
        p = &w;
        p -> pr_list();
    }
    p -> pr_list();
}
```

Notice that there is an inner block in main. That block is included to test that the destructor is invoked upon block exit, returning storage associated with w to free store. The output of this program is

```
B -> A ->
###
A ->
###
A ->
###

###
```

The first pr_list call prints the two-element list storing B and A. After a del operation is performed, the list contains one element storing A. The outer block pointer to list p is assigned the address of the list variable w. When the list is accessed through p in the inner block, it prints A. After block exit the same print command prints the empty list. This output shows that the destructor works at block exit on the variable w.

4.7. Two-Dimensional Arrays

Traditional C does not have authentic higher dimensional arrays. Instead, the programmer must be careful to map such an abstract data structure into a pointer to pointer to . . . base type. In C++ the programmer can implement flexible safe dynamic higher dimensional arrays. We will demonstrate this by implementing a two-dimensional array type `matrix`. The observant reader will notice the strong parallels with the class `vect`.

```
//A two-dimensional safe array type matrix
#include <stream.h>

class matrix {
    int**   p;
    int     s1, s2;
public:
    int     ub1, ub2;
    matrix(int d1, int d2);
    ~matrix();
    int& element(int i, int j);
};
```

The type `matrix` has a size for each dimension and a corresponding public upper bound. The hidden representation uses the pointer to pointer to `int` type. This will store the base address of a vector of pointers to `int` that in turn store a base address for each row vector of the `matrix` type.

```
matrix::matrix(int d1, int d2)
{
    if (d1 < 0 || d2 < 0) {
        cerr << "illegal matrix size "
            << d1 << " by " << d2 << "\n";
        exit(1);
    }
    s1 = d1;
    s2 = d2;
    p = new int*[s1];
    for (int i = 0; i < s1; ++i)
        p[i] = new int[s2];
    ub1 = s1 - 1;
    ub2 = s2 - 1;
}
```

```
matrix::~matrix()
{
   for (int i = 0;  i <= ub1;  ++i)
      delete p[i];
   delete p;
}
```

What is novel here are the ways in which the constructor and destructor work. The constructor allocates a vector of pointer to `int`. The number of elements in this vector is the value of `s1`. Next the constructor iteratively allocates a vector of `int` pointed at by each element `p[i]`. Therefore there is space for `s1 * s2` integers allocated from free store, and additionally the space for `s1` pointers is allocated from free store. The destructor deallocates store in the reverse order. All of this generalizes to higher dimensions.

Obtaining the reference to (lvalue of) an element in this two-dimensional array requires two index arguments.

```
int& matrix::element(int i, int j)
{
   if (i < 0 || i > ub1 || j < 0 || j > ub2) {
      cerr << "illegal matrix index "
           << ub1 << ", " << ub2 << "\n";
      exit(1);
   }
   return (p[i][j]);
}
```

Both arguments are tested to see that they are in range. This is a generalization of the one index case.

4.8. The `this` Pointer

The keyword `this` denotes an implicitly declared self-referential pointer. It can be used in any non-static member function. A simple illustration of its use is as follows:

```
// Use of the this pointer

#include <stream.h>

class X {
    char c;      // X* const this  is implicit
public:
    void init(char b) { c = b; }
    char valc() { return (this -> c); }
    unsigned where_am_I() { return ((unsigned)this); }
};

main()
{
    X  a, b, c;
    a.init('A');
    b.init('B');
    c.init('C');
    cout << a.valc() << " is at " << a.where_am_I() << "\n";
    cout << b.valc() << " is at " << b.where_am_I() << "\n";
    cout << c.valc() << " is at " << c.where_am_I() << "\n";
}
```

The member function valc() uses the implicitly provided pointer this to access the member variable c. Of course, it is unnecessary because the member variable is directly available. The member function where_am_I() returns the address of the given object.

Early C++ systems allowed memory management for objects to be controlled by assignment to the this pointer. Such code is obsolete because the this pointer is non-modifiable.

4.9. Summary

1. A constructor is a member function whose name is the same as the class name. It *constructs* objects of the class type. This process may involve initializing data members and allocating free store using new.

2. A destructor is a member function whose name is the class name preceded by the character ~. Its usual purpose is to *destroy* values of the class type, typically by using delete. A variable of a class having a destructor cannot be a member of a union.

3. A class with constructors that has a constructor with a void argument list can be the base type of an array declaration. A class with constructors that always require parameters cannot be the base type of an array declaration. Not all classes can have constructors. A variable of a class having a constructor cannot be a member of a union. A class with a static member cannot have a constructor.

4. An example of a class with both a constructor and destructor is

```
class stack {
    char* s;
    int    max_len;
    int    top;
public:
    stack(int size) { s = new char[size];
                           max_len = size; top = 0; }
    ~stack(void) { delete s; }
         . . .
};
```

5. A constructor of the form

   type: : *type* (*type*& x)

   is used to perform copying of one *type* value into another when:

   A *type* variable is initialized by a *type* value.
   A *type* value is passed as an argument in a function.
   A *type* value is returned from a function.

   In older C++ systems, if this constructor is not present, then these operations are bitwise copy. In newer systems, the default is member-by-member assignment of value.

6. Classes with constructors having an empty argument list can have a derived array type. For example, in Section 4.4

```
vect a[5];
```

is a declaration that uses the empty argument constructor to create an array a of five objects, each of which is a size 10 vect.

7. A class having members whose type requires a constructor may have these specified after the argument list for its own constructor. The constructor has a comma-separated list, following a colon, of constructor calls. The constructor is invoked by using the member name followed by a parenthesized argument list. In early versions of the C++ language, the order of constructor invocation was unspecified. In newer versions the order is as written in the comma-separated list, followed by any default initializations.

8. A singly linked list is the prototype of many useful dynamic data structures called *self-referential* structures. A linked list is like a clothes line on which the data elements hang sequentially. The head of the line is the only immediate access point, and items can readily be added to or deleted from this point.

9. The value 0 is called the *null pointer constant*. It can be assigned to any pointer type. In linked lists it typically denotes the empty list or end-of-list value.

10. The keyword this denotes an implicitly declared self-referential pointer. The this pointer can only be used inside a class member function to refer to non-static members.

4.10. Exercises

1. Discuss why constructors are almost always public member functions. What goes wrong if they are private?

2. Write a member function for the class mod_int

```
void add_to(int i);    //add i to v modulo 60.
```

It should add the number of seconds in i to the current value of v, while retaining the modulo 60 feature of v.

3. Run the following program and explain its behavior. Placing debugging information inside constructors and destructors is a very useful step in developing efficient and correct classes.

```
//Constructors and destructors invoked

#include <stream.h>

class A {
    int xx;
public:
    A(int n) { xx = n;
                cout << form("A(int %d) called\n", n); }
    A(double y) { xx = y + 0.5;
                cout << form("A(fl %f) called\n", y); }
    ~A() { cout << form("~A() called A::xx = %d\n", xx); }
};

main()
{
    cout << "enter main\n";
    int x = 14;
    double y = 17.3;
    A z(11), zz(11.5), zzz(0);

    zzz = A(x);
    zzz = A(y);
    cout << "exit main\n";
}
```

4. Add an empty parameter list constructor for class A.

```
A() { xx = 0; cout << "A() called\n"; }
```

Now modify the previous program by declaring a vector of type A

```
A d[5];    //declares a vector of 5 elements of type A
```

Assign the values 0, 1, 2, 3, and 4 to the data member xx of each d[i]. Run the program and explain its behavior.

5. Use the stack type in Section 4.1 in this exercise and include the empty argument constructor to allocate a stack of 100 elements. Write a program that swaps the contents of two stacks, using a vector

of stacks to accomplish the job. The two stacks will be the first two stacks in the vector. One method would be to use four stacks: st[0], st[1], st[2] and st[3]. Push the contents of st[1] into st[2]. Push the contents of st[0] into st[3]. Push the contents of st[3] into st[1]. Push the contents of st[2] into st[0]. Verify that the stacks have their contents in the same order by implementing a print function that outputs all elements in the stack. Can this be done with three stacks only?

6. Add a constructor to the type stack with the following prototype:

```
stack::stack(char* c);    //initialize from string array
```

7. Use the string type in Section 4.3 in this exercise and code the following member functions:

```
//strcmp is negative if s < s1,
//        is 0 if s == s1,
//        and is positive if s > s1
//        where s is the implicit string argument
int string::strcmp(string& s1);

//strrev  reverses the implicit string argument
void string::strrev();

//print  is overloaded to print the first n characters
void string::print(int n);
```

8. Write a function that swaps two strings. Use it and string::strcmp from the previous exercise to write a program that will sort an array of strings.

9. Use the vect type in Section 4.4 in this exercise and code the following member functions:

```
//adds up all the element values and returns their sum
int vect::sumelem();

//prints all the elements
void vect::print();

//adds two vectors into a third  v(implicit) = v1 + v2
void vect::add(vect& v1, vect& v2);

//adds two vectors and returns  v(implicit) + v1
vect vect::add(vect& v1);
```

10. Write a further constructor for `vect` that accepts an `int` array and its size and constructs a `vect` with these initial values.

```
vect::vect(int* d, int sz);
```

11. Try to benchmark the speed differences between safe arrays as represented by `class vect` and ordinary integer arrays. Repeatedly run an ordinary element summation routine on `int a[10000]` and one using the `vect a(10000)`. Time your trials.

12. Define the class `multi_v` as follows:

```
class multi_v {
    vect a, b, c;
    int  size;
public:
    int  ub;
    multi_v(int i):a(i), b(i), c(i) { size = i;
                                      ub = size -1; }
    void assign(int ind, int i, int j, int k);
    void retrieve(int ind, int& i, int& j, int& k);
    void print(int ind);
};
```

Write and test code for each member function: `assign`, `retrieve`, and `print`. The function `assign` should assign `i`, `j`, and `k` to `a[ind]`, `b[ind]`, and `c[ind]`, respectively. The function `retrieve` does the inverse of `assign`. The function `print` should print the three values `a[ind]`, `b[ind]`, and `c[ind]`.

13. Use the `list` type in Section 4.6 in this exercise and code the following member functions:

```
//list a constructor whose initializer is a char array
list::list(char* c);

//length returns the length of the list
int list::length();

//return the number of elements whose data value is c
int list::count_c(char c);
```

14. Write a member function `append` that will add a list to the rear of the implicit list argument, then clear the appended string by zeroing the head.

    ```
    void list::append(list& e);
    ```

15. Write a member function `copy` that will copy a list.

    ```
    //the implicit argument ends up a copy of e
    void list::copy(list& e);
    ```

    Be sure you destroy the implicit list before you do the copy.

16. Use the `list` type and add the equivalent five member functions that give you stack functions.

    ```
    reset    push    pop   top_of   empty
    ```

17. The following function is a traditional C two-dimensional matrix multiply.

    ```
    void mmpy(int a[M][N], int b[N][R], int c[M][R])
    {
        int  i, j, k, t;

        for (i = 0; i < M; ++i)
            for (j = 0; j < R; ++j) {
                t = 0;
                for (k = 0; k < N; ++k)
                    t += a[i][k] * b[k][j];
                c[i][j] = t;
            }
    }
    ```

    Write the corresponding function for `class matrix`

    ```
    void matrix::mmpy(matrix& a, matrix& b);
    ```

    where the result of the multiply is the implicit matrix argument.

18. Construct a three-dimensional safe array type called v_3_d.

```
//Implementation of a three-dimensional safe array
class v_3_d {
    int*** p;
    int    s1, s2, s3;
public:
    int    ub1, ub2, ub3;
    v_3_d(int l1, int l2, int l3);
    ~v_3_d();
    int& element(int i, int j, int k);
    void print();
};
```

Initialize and print a three-dimensional array.

CHAPTER 5

Operator Overloading and Conversions

This chapter describes operator overloading and conversions of data types. Overloading operators gives them new meanings for ADTs. The ADT can then be used in much the same way as a built-in type. For example, the expression a + b will have a different meaning depending on the types of the variables a and b. The expression could mean string concatenation, complex number addition, or integer addition depending, respectively, on whether the variables were the ADT string, the ADT complex, or the built-in type int. Mixed type expressions are also possible by defining conversion functions. This chapter also discusses friend functions and how they are crucial to operator overloading.

113

5.1. The Traditional Conversions

An arithmetic expression such as x + y has both a value and a type. For example, if x and y are both variables of the same type, say int, then x + y is also an int. However, if x and y are of different types, then x + y is a *mixed expression*. Suppose x is a short and y is an int. Then the value of x is converted to an int, and the expression x + y has type int. Note carefully that the value of x as stored in memory is unchanged. It is only a temporary copy of x that is converted during the computation of the value of the expression. Now suppose that both x and y are of type short. Even though x + y is not a mixed expression, automatic conversions again take place; both x and y are promoted to int and the expression is of type int. The general rules are straightforward.

Automatic conversion in an arithmetic expression x *op* y

First:
    Any char or short is promoted to int.
    Any unsigned char or unsigned short is promoted to unsigned.

Second:
    If after the first step the expression is of mixed type, then according to the hierarchy of types

    int < unsigned < long < unsigned long < float < double

    the operand of lower type is promoted to that of the higher type and the value of the expression has that type.

To illustrate implicit conversion, we first make the following declarations:

```
char c;       double d;     float f;      int i;
long lg;      short s;      unsigned u;
```

Now we can list a variety of mixed expressions along with their corresponding types:

Expression	Type	Expression	Type
c - s / i	int	u * 3 - i	unsigned
u * 3.0 - i	double	f * 3 - i	float
c + 1	int	3 * s * 1g	long
c + 1.0	double	d + s	double

In addition to automatic conversions in mixed expressions, an automatic conversion also can occur across an assignment. For example

```
d = i
```

causes the value of i, which is an int, to be converted to a dou015 and then assigned to d; double is the type of the expression as a whole. A promotion or widening such as d = i will usually be well behaved, but a narrowing or demotion such as i = d can lose information. Here, the fractional part of d will be discarded. Precisely what happens in each case is machine-dependent.

In addition to implicit conversions, which can occur across assignments and in mixed expressions, there are explicit conversions called *casts*. If i is an int, then

```
(double) i
```

will cast the value of i so that the expression has type double. The variable i itself remains unchanged. Casts can be applied to expressions. Some examples are

```
(char) ('A' + 1.0)
x = (float) ((int) y + 1)
(double) (x = 77)
```

The cast operator (*type*) is a unary operator having the same precedence and right-to-left associativity as other unary operators. Thus the expression

```
(float) i + 3
```
is equivalent to   `((float) i) + 3`

because the cast operator (*type*) has higher precedence than +.

These conversions are all found in C. In C++, we also have implicit pointer conversions. As we mentioned in Chapter 2 any pointer type can be converted to a generic pointer of type void*. Other pointer conversions include: the name of an array is a pointer to its base element;

the null pointer value can be converted to any type; the type function returning x is converted to pointer to function. C++ is generally stricter than traditional C and does not allow mixing of pointer types unless they are correctly cast.

5.2. ADT Conversions

Explicit type conversion of an expression is necessary when either the implicit conversions are not desired or the expression will not otherwise be legal. Traditional C casts are augmented in C++ by a functional notation as a syntactic alternative. C++ has as one aim: the integration of user-defined ADTs and built-in types. To achieve this, there is a mechanism for having a member function provide an explicit conversion.
A functional notation of the form

type-name   (expression)

is equivalent to a cast. The type must be expressible as an identifier. Thus, the two expressions

```
x = float(i);      //C++ functional notation
x = (float) i;
```

are equivalent. The expression

```
p = (int*) q;      //legal cast
```

cannot be directly expressed functionally as

```
p = int*(q);      //illegal
```

However, a typedef can be used to achieve this result:

```
typedef  int*  int_ptr;
p = int_ptr(q);
```

Functional notation is the preferred style.

A constructor of one argument is de facto a type conversion from the argument's type to the constructor's class type. In Section 4.3 the string type had a constructor

```
string(char* p) { len = strlen(p);
                s = new char[len + 1]; strcpy(s, p); }
```

This is automatically a type transfer from char* to string. It is available both explicitly and implicitly. Explicitly it is used as a conversion operation in either cast or functional form. Thus

```
string s;
char*  logo = "Geometrics Inc";

s = string(logo);     //performs conversion then assignment
```

and

```
s = logo;             //implicit invocation of conversion
```

both work.

These are conversions from an already defined type to a user-defined type. However, it is not possible for the user to add a constructor to a built-in type such as int or double. In the string example, one may also want a conversion from string to char*. This can be done by defining a special conversion function inside the string class, as follows:

```
operator char*() { return (s); }    //char* s is a member
```

The general form of such a member function is

```
operator type()  { . . . }
```

These conversions occur implicitly in assignment expressions, in arguments to functions, and in values returned from functions.

5.3. Overloading and Function Selection

Overloaded functions are an important addition in C++. The overload meaning is selected by matching the argument list of the function call to the argument list of the function declaration. When an overloaded function is invoked, the compiler must have a selection algorithm with which to pick the appropriate function. The algorithm that accomplishes this depends on what type conversions are available. A best match must be unique. It must be best on at least one argument and as good on all other arguments as any other match.

The matching algorithm for each argument is as follows:

Overloaded Function Selection Algorithm

1. Use an exact match if found.

2. Try standard type conversions.

3. Try user-defined conversions.

4. Use a match to ellipsis if found.

Let us write an overloaded function `greater` and follow our algorithm for various invocations. In this example the user type `complex` is available.

```
//overloading functions

#include <stream.h>
double sqrt(double);

class complex {
    double real, imag;
public:
    complex(double r) { real = r; imag = 0; }
    void assign(double r, double i) { real = r; imag = i; }
    void print() { cout << real << " + " << imag << "i "; }
    operator double() {return(sqrt(real * real + imag * imag));}
};

inline int     greater(int i, int j)
               { return ( i > j ? i : j); }
inline double  greater(double x, double y)
               { return ( x > y ? x : y); }
inline complex greater(complex w, complex z)
               { return ( w > z ? w : z); }
```

```
main()
{
    int      i = 10, j = 5;
    double   x = 7.0
    float    y = 14.5
    complex w(0), z(0), zmax(0);

    w.assign(x, y);
    z.assign(i, j);
    cout << form("compare %d  and  %d  greater is %d\n",
                    i, j, greater(i,j));
    cout << form("compare %g  and  %d  greater is %g\n",
                    x, y, greater(x,y));
    cout << "compare " << y << "  and   ";
    z.print();
    cout << "  greater is " << greater(y, double(z)) << "\n";
    zmax = greater(w, z);
    cout << "compare ";
    w.print();
    cout << "  and   ";
    z.print();
    cout << "  greater is   ";
    zmax.print();
    cout << "\n\n";
}
```

The output from this program is:

```
compare 10  and   5  greater is 10
compare 7  and  14.5  greater is 14.5
compare 14.5  and  10 + 5i    greater is 14.5
compare 7 + 14.5i   and   10 + 5i   greater is  7 + 14.5i
```

A variety of conversion rules, both implicit and explicit, are being applied. We explain these in the following dissection.

■ DISSECTION OF THE *overloading* PROGRAM

```
complex(double r) { real = r; imag = 0; }
```

● This constructor provides a conversion from `double` to `complex`.

```
operator double() {return(sqrt(real * real + imag * imag));}
```

- This member function provides a conversion from complex to double.

```
inline int     greater(int i, int j)
               { return ( i > j ? i : j); }
inline double  greater(double x, double y)
               { return ( x > y ? x : y); }
inline complex greater(complex w, complex z)
               { return ( w > z ? w : z); }
```

- Three distinct functions are overloaded. The most interesting has complex type for its argument list variables and its return type. The conversion member function operator double is required to evaluate w > z. The complex variables w and z are converted to double. Later in this chapter we will discuss overloading operators, a construct that will allow us to provide new meanings to existing C++ operators. No conversion is necessary for the return type.

```
w.assign(x, y);
z.assign(i, j);
```

- The first invocation of the member function assign requires the float argument x to be converted to double. The double argument y requires no conversion. The second invocation has both arguments as int, requiring conversion. Integer arguments are assignment compatible with double.

```
cout << form("compare %d  and  %d  greater is %d\n",
             i, j, greater(i,j));
cout << form("compare %g  and  %d  greater is %g\n",
             x, y, greater(x,y));
```

- The first statement selects the first definition of greater because of the exact match rule. The second statement selects the second definition of greater because of the use of a standard widening conversion float to double. The value of variable x is widened to double.

```
cout << "  greater is " << greater(y, double(z)) << "\n";
```

- The second definition of `greater` is selected because of the exact match rule. The explicit conversion `double(z)` is necessary to avoid ambiguity. The function call

```
greater(y, z);
```

   would have two available conversions to achieve a match. The user-defined conversion of `double` to `complex` for the argument y matches the third definition. The user-defined conversion from `complex` to `double` for the argument z matches the second definition. This violates the uniqueness provision for matching when user-specified conversions are involved.

```
zmax = greater(w, z);
```

- An exact match for definition three.

5.4. Friend Functions

The keyword `friend` is a function specifier. It gives a nonmember function access to the hidden members of the class. Its use is a method of escaping the strict strong typing and data hiding restrictions of C++. However, we must have a good reason for escaping these restrictions, as they are both important to reliable programming. This feature of the C++ language is controversial.

One reason for using `friend` functions is that some functions need privileged access to more than one class. A second reason is that `friend` functions pass all their arguments through the argument list, and each argument value is subject to assignment-compatible conversions. Conversions would apply to a class variable passed explicitly and would be especially useful in cases of operator overloading, as seen in the next section.

A `friend` function must appear inside the class declaration to which it is a friend. The function is prefaced by the keyword `friend` and can appear in either the public or private part of the class without affecting its meaning. Member functions of one class can be `friend` functions of another class. In this case they are written in the friend's class using the scope resolution operator to qualify its function name. If all member functions of one class are `friend` functions of a second class, this can be specified by writing `friend class` *class name*.

The following declarations illustrate the syntax:

```
class tweedledee {
    . . .
    friend void alice();              //friend function
    int         cheshire();           //member function
    . . .
};

class tweedledum {
    . . .
    friend int tweedledee::cheshire();
    . . .
};

class tweedledumber {
    . . .
    friend class tweedledee;    //all member functions
                                //of tweedledee have access
    . . .
};
```

Consider the `class matrix` and the `class vect` in Chapter 4. A function multiplying a vector by a matrix as represented by these two classes could be written efficiently if it had access to the private members of both classes. It would be a `friend` function of both classes. In our discussion in Chapter 4, safe access was provided to the elements of `vect` and `matrix` with their respective member function `element`. One could write a function using this access that would multiply without requiring `friend` status. However, the price in functional call overhead and array bounds checking would make such a matrix multiply unnecessarily inefficient.

```
    class matrix;                          //forward reference

    class vect {
        int*        p;
        int         size;
        friend vect mpy(vect& v, matrix& m);
    public:
        . . .
    };

    class matrix {
        int**       p;
        int         s1, s2;
        friend vect mpy(vect& v, matrix& m);
    public:
        . . .
    };

    vect mpy(vect& v, matrix& m)
    {
        if (v.size != m.s1) {       //incorrect sizes
            cerr << "multiply failed - sizes incorrect "
                 << v.size << " and " << m.s1 << "\n";
            exit(1);
        }
        //use privileged access to p in both classes
        vect ans(m.s2);
        for (int i = 0; i <= m.ub2; ++i) {
            ans.p[i] = 0;
            for (int j = 0; j <= m.ub1; ++j)
                ans.p[i] += v.p[j] * m.p[j][i];
        }
        return (ans);
    }
```

A minor point is the necessity of an empty declaration of the class matrix. This is necessary because the function mpy must appear in both classes and it uses each class as an argument type.

Friends are controversial because they break through the encapsulating wall surrounding private members of classes. The OOP paradigm is that objects (in C++ these are class variables) should be accessed through their public members. Only member functions should have access to the hidden implementation of the ADT. This is a neat, orderly design principle. The friend function, however, straddles this boundary. It is neither fish nor fowl. It has access to private members but is not itself a member function. It can be used to provide quick fixes to code that needs access to the implementation details of a class. But the mechanism is easily abused. However, as in the previous example, some coding situations require its use.

5.5. Overloading Operators

The keyword `operator` is used to define a type conversion member function. It is also used to overload the built-in C operators. Just as a function name, such as `print`, can be given a variety of meanings that depend on its arguments, so can an operator, such as `+`, be given additional meanings. Overloading operators allows infix expressions of both ADTs and built-in types to be written. It is an important notational convenience and in many instances leads to shorter and more readable programs.

The previous section's `mpy` function could have been written as:

```
vect operator* (vect& v, matrix& m)
    . . .
```

If this had been done, and if `r` and `s` were `vect` and `t` was a `matrix`, then the natural looking expression

```
r = s * t;
```

would invoke the multiply function. This replaces the functional notation

```
r = mpy(s, t);
```

Although meanings can be added to operators, their associativity and precedence remain the same. For example, the multiplication operator will remain of higher precedence than the add operator. The operator precedence table for C++ is included in Appendix B. Almost all operators can be overloaded. The exceptions are the member operator `.`, the member object selector operator `.*`, the ternary conditional express operator `?:`, the `sizeof` operator, and the scope resolution operator `::`. Furthermore, the autoincrement and autodecrement operators, `++` and `--`, cannot have distinct prefix and postfix meanings.

Available operators include all the arithmetic, logical, comparison, equality, assignment, and bit operators. The subscript operator `[]` and the function call `()` can also be overloaded. It is also possible to overload `new` and `delete`.

5.6. Unary Operator Overloading

We will continue our discussion of operator overloading by demonstrating how to overload unary operators, such as !, ++, ~, and []. For this purpose we develop the class clock, which can be used to store time as days, hours, minutes, and seconds. We will develop familiar operations on this clock.

```
class clock {
    unsigned int  tot_secs, secs, mins, hours, days;
public:
    clock(unsigned int i);       //constructor and conversion
    void print();                //formatted printout
    void tick();                 //add one second
    clock operator ++() { this -> tick(); return(*this); }
};
```

This class overloads the autoincrement operator. The overloaded operator is a member function and can be invoked on its implicit single argument. The member function tick adds one second to the implicit argument of the overloaded ++ operator.

```
inline clock::clock(unsigned int i)
{
    tot_secs = i;
    secs = tot_secs % 60;
    mins = (tot_secs / 60) % 60;
    hours = (tot_secs / 3600) % 24;
    days = tot_secs / 86400;
}

void clock::tick()
{
    clock  temp = clock(++tot_secs);

    secs = temp.secs;
    mins = temp.mins;
    hours = temp.hours;
    days = temp.days;
}
```

The constructor performs the usual conversions from tot_secs to days, hours, minutes, and seconds. For example, there are 86,400 seconds in a day, and therefore integer division by this constant gives the whole number of days. The member function tick constructs clock temp, which adds one second to the total time. The constructor acts as a conversion function that properly updates the time.

The overloaded member function ++ also updates the implicit `clock` variable, but returns the updated value as well. It could have been coded in the same way as `tick`, except that the statement

```
return(temp);
```

would be added.

Adding the following code, we can test our functions:

```
void clock::print()
{
   cout << days << " d :" << hours << " h :"
        << mins << " m :" << secs << " s\n";
}

main()
{
   clock t1(59), t2(172799);   //min - 1 sec and 2 days - 1 sec
   cout << "initial times are\n";
   t1.print();
   t2.print();
   ++t1;   ++t2;               //t1++; t2++ are also possible
   cout << "after one second times are\n";
   t1.print();
   t2.print();
}
```

The output is

```
initial times are
0 d :0 h :0 m :59 s
1 d :23 h :59 m :59 s
after one second times are
0 d :0 h :1 m :0 s
2 d :0 h :0 m :0 s
```

It would have been possible to overload ++ using a `friend` function as follows:

```
friend clock clock::operator ++(clock& cl)
                    { cl.tick(); return(cl); }
```

Note, since the clock variable must advance by one second, we call it by reference. The decision to choose between a `friend` representation and a member function representation typically depends on whether or not implicit conversion operations are available and desirable. Explicit argument passing, as in `friend` functions, allows the argument to be automatically coerced if necessary and possible.

5.7. Binary Operator Overloading

We continue with our `clock` example and show how to overload binary operators. Basically the same principles hold. When a binary operator is overloaded using a member function, it has as its first argument the implicitly passed class variable and as its second argument the lone argument list parameter. Friend functions or ordinary functions have both arguments specified in the parameter list. Of course ordinary functions cannot access private members.

Let us create an adding operation for type `clock` that will add two values together.

```
class clock {
    . . .
    friend clock operator +(clock c1, clock c2);
};

clock operator +(clock c1, clock c2)
{
    unsigned total_sec = c1.tot_secs + c2.tot_secs;
    clock temp = total_sec;
    return (temp);
}
```

Both arguments are specified explicitly. They are both candidates for assignment conversions. The line of code

```
clock temp = total_sec;
```

uses the constructor to convert `total_sec` into a `clock` value. This could have also been written

```
clock temp(total_sec);
```

In contrast, let us overload binary minus with a member function.

```
class clock {
    . . .
    clock operator -(clock c);
};

clock clock::operator -(clock c)
{
    unsigned total_sec = tot_secs - c.tot_secs;
    clock temp = total_sec;
    return (temp);
}
```

Remember that there is an implicit first argument. This takes some getting used to.

We will define a multiplication operation as a binary operation with one argument an unsigned int and the second argument a clock variable. The operation will require the use of a friend function. A member function must have the first argument from its class.

```
clock operator *(unsigned int m, clock c)
{
    unsigned total_sec = m * c.tot_secs;
    clock temp = total_sec;
    return (temp);
}
```

This requirement forces the multiplication to have a fixed ordering that is type-dependent. To avoid this, it is common practice to write a second overloaded function:

```
clock operator *(clock c, unsigned int m)
    . . .
```

5.8. Overloading Assignment and Subscripting Operators

In C++ there are reference declarations. In effect, such type modifiers produce lvalues. On the right side of an assignment expression, an lvalue is automatically dereferenced. On the left side of an assignment expression, it specifies where an appropriate value is to be stored. Both subscripting and assignment make use of these properties of lvalues. For

ADTs, we must define such expressions unless satisfactory defaults are available. We will reimplement the class vect from Section 4.4, extending its functionality by applying operator overloading.

The reimplemented class will have several improvements to make it both safer and more useful. A constructor that converts an ordinary integer array to a safe array will be added. This will allow us to develop code using safe arrays and later run the same code efficiently on ordinary arrays. The public data member ub has been changed to a member function. This prevents a user from inadvertently introducing a program error by modifying the member. Finally, the subscript operator [] is overloaded and replaces the member function element.

```
//A safe array type vect with [] overloaded
#include <stream.h>

class vect {
    int* p;                             //base pointer
    int size;                           //number of elements
public:
    //constructors and destructor
    vect();                             //create a size 10 array
    vect(int n);                        //create a size n array
    vect(vect& v);                      //initialization by vect
    vect(int a[], int n);               //initialization by array
    ~vect() { delete p; }
    //other member functions
    int ub() { return (size - 1); }   //upper bound
    int& operator [](int i);            //range checked element
};

vect::vect()
{
    size = 10;
    p = new int[size];
}

vect::vect(int n)
{
    if (n <= 0) {
        cerr << "illegal vect size: " << n << "\n";
        exit(1);
    }
    size = n;
    p = new int[size];
}
```

```
vect::vect(int a[], int n)
{
   if (n <= 0) {
      cerr << "illegal vect size: " << n << "\n";
      exit(1);
   }
   size = n;
   p = new int[size];
   for (int i = 0; i < size; ++i)
      p[i] = a[i];
}

vect::vect(vect& v)
{
   size = v.size;
   p = new int[size];
   for (int i = 0; i < size; ++i)
      p[i] = v.p[i];
}

int& vect::operator [](int i)
{
   if (i < 0 || i > ub()) {
      cerr << "illegal vect index: " << i << "\n";
      exit(1);
   }
   return (p[i]);
}
```

An overloaded subscript operator can have any return type and any argument list type. However, it is good style to maintain the consistency between a user-defined meaning and standard usage. Thus a most common function prototype is:

   class name& operator [] (*integral type*);

A reference value is returned in such functions that can be used on either side of an assignment expression.

It is also convenient to be able to assign one array to another. The user can specify the behavior of assignment by overloading it. It is good style to maintain consistency with standard usage. The following member function overloads assignment for class vect:

```
vect& vect::operator =(vect& v)
{
   int s = (size < v.size) ? size : v.size;

   if (v.size != size)
      cerr << "copying different size arrays "
           << size << " and " << v.size << "\n";
   for (int i = 0; i < s; ++i)
      p[i] = v.p[i];
   return (*this);
}
```

■ DISSECTION OF THE *vect::operator =(vect& v)* FUNCTION

```
vect& vect::operator =(vect& v)
```

- The operator = function returns reference to vect and has one explicit argument of type reference to vect. The first argument of the assignment operator is the implicit argument. The function could have been written to return void, but then it would not have allowed multiple assignment.

```
int s = (size < v.size) ? size : v.size;
```

- The smaller size will be used in the element-by-element assignment. This function will allow a smaller array to have its contents copied into the beginning of a larger array. When assigning from the larger array, it will use only as many elements as are in the smaller array.

```
if (v.size != size)
   cerr << "copying different size arrays "
        << size << " and " << v.size << "\n";
```

- A warning to the user in case this use was inadvertent.

```
for (int i = 0; i < s; ++i)
    p[i] = v.p[i];
return (*this);
```

- The explicit argument v.p[] will be the right-hand side of the assignment; the implicit argument, as represented by p[], will be the left-hand side of the assignment. The self-referential pointer is dereferenced and passed back as the value of the expression. This allows multiple assignment with right-to-left associativity to be defined.

Expressions of type vect can be evaluated by overloading in appropriate ways the various arithmetic operators. As an example, let us overload binary plus to mean element-by-element addition of two vect variables.

```
vect vect::operator +(vect& v)
{
    int s = (size < v.size) ? size : v.size;
    vect   sum(s);

    if (v.size != size)
        cerr << "adding different size arrays"
             << size << " and " << v.size << "\n";
    for (int i = 0; i < s; ++i)
        sum.p[i] = p[i] + v.p[i];
    return (sum);
}
```

Now with the class vect, as extended, all of the following expressions are meaningful:

```
a = b;                      //a, b are type vect
a = b = c;                  //a, b, c are type vect
a = vect(data, DSIZE);      //convert array data[DSIZE]
a = b + a;                  //assignment and addition
a = b + (c = a) + d;        //complicated expression
```

The class vect is a full-fledged ADT. It behaves and appears in client code much as any built-in type behaves and appears.

5.9. Summary

1. Overloading operators gives them new meanings for ADTs. The ADT can then be used in much the same way as a built-in type. For example, the expression a + b will have a different meaning depending on the types of the variables a and b. The expression could mean string concatenation, complex number addition, or integer addition depending, respectively, on whether the variables were the ADT string, the ADT complex, or the built-in type int. Mixed type expressions are also possible by defining conversion functions.

2. A functional notation of the form

    type-name   (expression)

    is equivalent to a cast. The type must be expressible as an identifier. Thus, the two expressions

    ```
    x = float(i);    //C++ functional notation
    x = (float) i;
    ```

    are equivalent.

3. A constructor of one argument is de facto a type conversion from the argument's type to the constructor's class type. A conversion from a user-specified type to a built-in type can be made by defining a special conversion function. The general form of such a member function is

    ```
    operator type() { . . . }
    ```

    These conversions occur implicitly in assignment expressions, in arguments to functions, and in values returned from functions.

4. Overloaded functions are an important addition in C++. Which overloaded function is to be invoked requires the matching of the invocation argument list to the declaration parameter list. The matching algorithm simplified is as follows:

    1. Use an exact match if found.
    2. Try standard type conversions.

3. Try user-defined conversions.

4. Use a match to ellipsis if found.

5. The keyword `friend` is a function specifier. It allows a nonmember function access to the hidden members of the class of which it is a friend. Its use is a method of escaping the strict strong typing and data hiding restrictions of C++.

6. The keyword `operator` is also used to overload the built-in C operators. Just as a function name, such as `print`, can be given a variety of meanings that depend on its arguments, so can an operator, such as `+`, be given additional meanings. Overloading operators allows infix expressions of both user types and built-in types to be written. The precedence and associativity remain fixed.

7. Operator overloading typically uses either member functions or friend functions because they both have privileged access. When a unary operator is overloaded using a member function, it has an empty argument list because the single operator argument is the implicit argument. When a binary operator is overloaded using a member function, it has as its first argument the implicitly passed class variable and as its second argument the lone argument list parameter. Friend functions or ordinary functions have both arguments specified in the parameter list.

8. An overloaded subscript operator can have any return type and any argument list type. However, it is good style to maintain the consistency between a user-defined meaning and standard usage. Thus a most common function prototype is:

class name& operator `[]` (*integral type*);

A reference value is returned in such functions that can be used on either side of an assignment expression.

5.10. Exercises

1. The following table has a variety of mixed type expressions. You are to fill in both the type the expression is converted to and its value when well defined.

Declarations and initializations		

int   i = 3, *p = &i;
char   c = 'b';
float x = 2.14, *q = &x;		

Expression	Type	Value
i + c		
x + i		
p + i		
p == & i		
* p - * q		
(int)x + i		

2. For the type `complex` provide a constructor that converts an `int` to a `complex`. Explain why this is redundant where a constructor from `double` has been provided. Write an explicit conversion that converts `complex` to `double` with the meaning that its value is its real component.

3. If the following line of code from the `greater` program

   ```
   cout << "  greater is " << greater(y, double(z)) << "\n";
   ```

   is replaced by

   ```
   cout << "  greater is " << greater(y, z) << "\n";
   ```

   what goes wrong?

4. Write a function that adds a `vect v` to a `matrix m`. The prototype to be added to `class matrix` and `class vect` is

   ```
   friend vect add(vect& v, matrix& m);
   ```

   The `vect v` will be added element by element to each row of `m`.

5. The class `complex` as defined in this chapter is:

```
class complex {
    double real, imag;
public:
    complex(double r) { real = r; imag = 0; }
    void assign(double r, double i) { real = r; imag = i; }
    void print() { cout << real << " + " << imag << "i "; }
    operator double()
            { return(sqrt(real * real + imag * imag)); }
};
```

We wish to augment it by overloading a variety of operators. For example, the member function `print` could be replaced by overloading the ~ operator:

```
void operator ~() { cout << real << " + " << imag << "i "; }
```

Rewrite this as a `friend` function. Also code and test a unary minus operator. It should return a `complex` whose value in each part is negated.

6. For the type `complex` write the following binary operator functions: add, multiply, and subtract. Each should return `complex`. Write two versions, a `friend` version and a member function version.

7. Write two `friend` functions

```
friend complex operator +(complex, double);
friend complex operator +(double, complex);
```

In the absence of a conversion from type `double` to type `complex`, both types are needed in order to allow completely mixed expressions of `complex` and `double`. Explain why writing one with an `int` parameter is unnecessary when these `friend` functions are available.

8. Overload assignment for `complex`. In the presence of the conversion operator for converting `complex` to `double`, what is the effect of assigning a `complex` to `double`?

9. Program a `class vec_complex` that is a safe array type whose element values are `complex`. Overload the operators + and * to mean element-by-element `complex` addition and dot-product of two `complex` vectors, respectively. For added efficiency you can make the `class vec_complex` a friend of `class complex`.

10. The following member function is a form of *iterator*:

```
int& vect::iterate()
{
    static int i = 0;
    i = i % size;
    return (p[i++]);
}
```

It is called an iterator because it returns each element value of a vect in sequence. Use it to write a print function that is not a member function and that writes out all element values of a given vect.

11. Exercise 10 has a serious limitation. By providing an iterator that is contained in the class, the element sequencing will not depend on the individual vect variable. Thus, if a and b are both vect variables, the first call of a.iterate() will get the first element of a and a subsequent call of b.iterate() will get the second element of b. So instead we will define a new class vect_iterator as follows:

```
class vect_iterator {
    int i;
public:
    vect_iterator() { i = 0; }
    int& iterate();
};
```

This class is to be a friend of vect. Write the code for iterate(). Then for each declaration of a vect there will be a corresponding declaration of its iterator. For example,

```
vect a(5), b(10);
vect_iterator it_a, it_b;
```

Use this to write a function that finds the maximum element value in a vect. *Hint*: If necessary read Section 8.5.

12. Define a new class matrix_iterator as the iterator that sequences through all elements of a matrix (Section 4.7). Use it to find the maximum element in a matrix.

13. Redo the string ADT of Section 4.3 by using operator overloading. The member function assign should be changed to become operator=.

The member function concat should be changed to become operator+. Also, overload operator[] to return the ith character in the string. If there is no such character, the value −1 is to be returned.

14. Redo the list ADT of Section 4.6 by using operator overloading. The member function add should be changed to become operator+. The member function del should be changed to become operator--. Also, overload operator[] to return the ith element in the list.

CHAPTER 6
Inheritance

This chapter describes inheritance in C++. Inheritance is the mechanism of *deriving* a new class from an old one. That is, the existing class can be added to or altered to create the derived class. Through inheritance, a hierarchy of related ADTs can be created that share code, a feature critical to the ability to reuse code. Inheritance is an important component of OOP.

Many useful data structures are variants of one another, and it is frequently tedious to produce the same code for each. A derived class inherits the description of the *base* class. It can then be altered by adding members, overloading existing member functions, and modifying access privileges. The usefulness of this concept can be seen by examining how taxonomic classification compactly summarizes large bodies of knowledge. For example, knowing the concept mammal and knowing that an elephant and mouse are both mammals allows our descriptions of them to be considerably more succinct than they would be otherwise. The root concept mammal contains the information that mammals are warm-blooded animals and higher vertebrates, and that they nourish their young using milk-producing mammary glands. This information is inherited by both the mouse and the elephant, but it is expressed only once: in the root class. In C++ terms, both elephant and mouse are derived from the base class mammal.

C++ supports virtual member functions. These are functions declared in the base class and overloaded in a derived class. An ADT hierarchy that is defined by inheritance creates a related set of user types, all of whose objects may be pointed at by a base class pointer. By accessing the virtual function through this pointer, C++ selects the appropriate overloaded function at run-time. The object being pointed at must carry around type information so that this distinction can be made dynamically, a feature typical of OOP code. Each object "knows" how it is to be acted on. We briefly touched on this in Section 1.7 and we will explain it in detail in this chapter.

The OOP design methodology becomes:

1. Decide on an appropriate set of ADTs.

2. Design in their relatedness and use inheritance to share code.

3. Use virtual functions to process related objects dynamically.

6.1. A Derived Class

A class can be derived from an existing class using the form:

```
class class-name :  (public|private) optional  base-class-name
{
    member declarations
};
```

As usual, the keyword class can be replaced by the keyword struct, with the usual implication that members are default public. The most complicated aspect of the derived class is the visibility of its inherited members. One of two keywords, public and private, can optionally be used to specify how the base class members are to be accessible to the derived class. We will explore this in detail in the next section.

An example of deriving a class is:

```
class student {
public:
    int    student_id;
    float  gpa;
    char   name[30];
    char   college[20];
    enum   {fresh, soph, junior, senior} year;
    char   major[10];
    void   print();
};

class grad_student:public student {
public:
    enum {ta, ra, fellowship, other} support;
    char dept[10];
    char thesis[80];
    void print();
};
```

In this example, grad_student is the derived class and student is the base class. The use of the keyword public following the colon in the derived class header means that the public members of student are to be public members of grad_student.

A derived class is a modification of the base class that inherits the public members of the base class. Thus, in the example of grad_student, the student members—student_id, gpa, name, college, year, major, and print —are inherited. Frequently, a derived class adds new members to the existing class members. This is the case with grad_student, which has three new data members and a redefined member function print. A derived class can also be restrictive. The derived class can change the visibility of members and it can alter their meanings.

6.2. public, private, and protected

The keywords public, private, and protected are available as visibility modifiers for class members. A public member is visible throughout its scope. A private member is visible to other member functions within its own class. A `protected` member is visible to other member functions within its class and any class immediately derived from it. These visibility modifiers can be used within a class declaration in any order and with any frequency. The usual style is:

```
class foo {
private:   //optional
    . . .
protected:
    . . .
public:
    . . .
};
```

This ordering is from least visible to most visible. In older compilers, where `private` and `protected` are not available, the ordering conforms to the omission of the keyword `private`. Where `protected` is unavailable, it is usual to have those members be `public`, although it is also possible to use `friend` functions in place of member functions for some purposes.

The visibility modifiers can be explicitly used in the class declaration header. If not used there, the default-inherited visibility for `class` is `private` and for `struct` is `public`. The recommended style is to always be explicit. The most frequent use is to make the base class publicly visible to the derived class. This was seen in the example of `grad_student` in the previous section. In `public` derivation, the derived class inherits both the `public` and `protected` members of the base class and retains these visibilities. Thus a `public` member of the base class is also a public member of the derived class. The private members of the base class are not accessible to the derived class. In `private` derivation, the derived class has access to both the `public` and `protected` members of the base class, but within the derived class they are considered `private`.

As can be seen, visibility modifiers in the header can be used to restrict access to members. It is possible to alter this for individual members in the derived class. If a member is transmitted to its derived class as `private`, this can be altered to `public` or `protected`, as in the following:

```
class b {
protected:
   int g;
public:
   int f;
   int h;
   . . .
};

class d : private b {   // f, g, h default to private
protected:
   b::g;      //g is converted to protected
public:
   b::f;      //f is converted to public
   . . .
};
```

In the same manner, a publicly transmitted member can be explicitly converted to `private` or `protected`. Such a declaration is called an *access declaration*. In general they cannot be used to prevent access to a member accessible in the base class, and they cannot be used to make members visible in the derived class that are inaccessible in the base class. The key design rule is to limit visibility as much as possible, which enhances the modularity of the resulting code. When using classes to implement an ADT, such as a stack, the public code should reflect the operations and functions that client code needs in using the ADT. The implementation details of an ADT, such as the choice of array or list to represent the stack, should be hidden in `private` and `protected` parts of the class.

6.3. A Derived Safe Array Type `vect_bnd`

In this section we will develop a safe array type that will be declared with both a lower bound and an upper bound. This style of array declaration was used in Algol 60 and PL/1. It will be derived from the `class` `vect` found in Section 5.8. The following program implements `class` `vect_bnd`, which allows safe array declaration using both lower and upper bound specification. It includes a simple test of the class in `main`.

```
//Derived safe array type vect_bnd
#include <stream.h>

class vect {
    int* p;                         //base pointer
    int  size;                      //number of elements
public:
    //constructors and destructor
    vect();                         //create a size 10 array
    vect(int n);                    //create a size n array
    vect(vect& v);                  //initialization by vect
    vect(int a[], int n);           //initialization by array
    ~vect(){ delete p; }
    //other member functions
    int  ub() { return (size - 1); }     //upper bound
    int& operator [](int i);        //a range checked element
    vect& operator =(vect& v);
    vect operator +(vect& v);
};

class vect_bnd : public vect {
    int l_bnd, u_bnd;
public:
    vect_bnd();
    vect_bnd(int, int);
    int& operator[](int);
    int  ub() { return (u_bnd); }
    int  lb() { return (l_bnd); }
};
```

The derived class vect_bnd has its own constructors, which will invoke the base class constructor. There is a special syntax to pass arguments from the derived class constructor back to the base class constructor.

function header : base-class-name $_{optional}$ (argument list)

This syntax is illustrated by the definitions of the derived class constructors.

```
vect_bnd::vect_bnd() :vect(10)
{
    //invokes the constructor vect(10);
    l_bnd = 0;
    u_bnd = 9;
}

vect_bnd::vect_bnd(int lb, int ub) :vect(ub - lb + 1)
{
    //invokes the constructor vect(ub - lb + 1);
    l_bnd = lb;
    u_bnd = ub;
}

int& vect_bnd::operator[](int i)
{
    if (i < l_bnd || u_bnd < i) {
        cerr << "index out of range: " << i << "\n";
        exit(1);
    }
    return (vect::operator[](i - l_bnd));
}

main()
{
    vect_bnd s(-5, 5);

    for (int i = s.lb(); i <= s.ub(); ++i) {
        s[i] = i;
        cout << i << "  ";
    }
    cout << "\n";
}
```

The declaration vect_bnd s(-5, 5) creates a one-dimensional safe array whose lower bound is −5 and whose upper bound is 5, a total of eleven elements. The output from this program is a series of values that is the index sequence of this array:

```
-5   -4   -3   -2   -1   0   1   2   3   4   5
```

■ DISSECTION OF THE *vect_bnd* CLASS

```
class vect_bnd : public vect {
    int l_bnd, u_bnd;
public:
    vect_bnd();
    vect_bnd(int, int);
    int& operator[](int);
    int  ub() { return (u_bnd); }
    int  lb() { return (l_bnd); }
};
```

- This is a publicly derived class incorporating the base class vect. The class vect has as private members the pointer p and the int variable size, which are not directly accessible to vect_bnd. They are implementation details that are hidden from clients of this class. The publicly accessible members of vect are also publicly accessible members of vect_bnd. The identifier ub is overloaded. The operator[] is also overloaded. Selection will depend on type matching unless explicit use of the scope resolution operator is made.

```
vect_bnd::vect_bnd() :vect(10)
{
    l_bnd = 0;
    u_bnd = 9;
}
```

```
vect_bnd::vect_bnd(int lb, int ub) :vect(ub - lb + 1)
{
    l_bnd = lb;
    u_bnd = ub;
}
```

- These are the two different constructors for vect_bnd. The first is an empty argument default constructor that creates a ten-element array. The parenthesized expression following the colon in the constructor header is the argument to the constructor for vect. The argument 10 is first passed back to the appropriate vect constructor and when executed creates a ten-element array. Then the body of this (the derived class) constructor is executed, assigning values to l_bnd and u_bnd. If a base class has a constructor, it is

invoked for the derived class. If the constructor needs an
argument list, this is provided in the derived class constructor heading as a parenthesized list following a colon. The
second constructor is a two-argument constructor whose
arguments are the bound's pair values for the safe array
variable. Note how they get used in the implicit argument
for the base class constructor.

```
int& vect_bnd::operator[](int i)
{
    if (i < l_bnd || u_bnd < i) {
        cerr << "index out of range: " << i << "\n";
        exit(1);
    }
    return  (vect::operator[](i - l_bnd));
}
```

- This function will accomplish range checked indexing into
  the safe array. Once the index is found to be legal, we wish
  to return the appropriate element's address. This is an address
  offset from the base pointer p that is inaccessible to this
  routine. However, the public member vect::operator[](int
  i) is accessible by use of the scope resolution operator.
  This base class member does have access to p and can
  return with the appropriate reference value. If vect:: were
  omitted in the return statement, the function would be a
  nonterminating recursion.

6.4. Typing Conversions and Visibility

A publicly derived class is a *subtype* of its base class. A variable of the
derived class can in many ways be treated as if it were the base class
type. A pointer whose type is pointer to base class can point to objects
having the derived class type. This can be confusing since subtle implicit
conversions are occurring between base and derived type, and it is sometimes difficult to follow what member is being accessed if the base and
derived class overloaded the same member name.

We will modify our earlier example of student and grad_student.

```
enum year {fresh, soph, junior, senior};
enum support {ta, ra, fellowship, other};

class student {
protected:
    int    student_id;
    float gpa;
public:
    student(int id, float g) { student_id = id; gpa = g; }
    char name[30];
    char college[20];
    year yr;
    char major[10];
    void print();
    void read();
};

class grad_student : public student {
    support  s;
public:
    grad_student(support x, int id, float g):(id, g) { s = x; }
    char dept[10];
    char thesis[80];
    void print();
    void read();
};
```

The grad_student is a publicly derived type whose base class is student. In the class student, the members student_id and gpa are protected. This makes them visible to the derived class but otherwise treated as private. The class grad_student has one private member s, with all other members public.

Both classes have constructors and both classes have overloaded read and print as member functions. The constructors act to initialize the non–publicly accessible data members. The constructor for grad_student, as is usual, invokes the constructor for student.

A reference to the derived class may be implicitly converted to a reference to the public base class. For example,

```
grad_student gs(ta, 201, 88.9);
student& rs = &gs;
```

In this case the variable rs is a reference to student. The base class of grad_student is student. Therefore this reference conversion is appropriate.

The `print` and `read` member functions are overloaded. We will implement the `print` functions and leave as an exercise the coding of the `read` functions.

```
void student::print()
{
    cout << form("%-30s %4d %-20s %-10s %1d %5.4f\n",
                   name, student_id, college, major, yr, gpa);
}

void grad_student::print()
{
    student::print();
    cout << form("%-10s %2d\n%-79s\n", dept, s, thesis);
}
```

For `grad_student::print` to invoke the `student::print` function, the scope-resolved identifier `student::print` must be used. Otherwise, there will be an infinite loop. To see which versions of these functions get called and to demonstrate some of the conversion relationships between base and publicly derived classes, we write a simple test program.

```
//Test pointer conversion rules.
#include "stud.h"   //include relevant declarations

main()
{
    student        s1(100, 87.6), s2(101, 67.0);
    student*       ps;
    grad_student   gs1(ta, 200, 88.8);
    grad_student*  pgs;

    ps = &s1;
    strcpy(ps -> name, "Mae Pohl");
    ps -> print();
    ps = pgs = &gs1;
    strcpy(ps -> name, "Morris Pohl");
    strcpy(pgs -> dept, "pharmacy");
    strcpy(pgs -> thesis, "Pharmacies as retail outlets.");
    ps -> print();
    pgs -> print();     //grad_student::print
}
```

This function declares both class variables and pointers to them. The conversion rule is that a pointer to a publicly derived class may be converted to a pointer to its base class. In our example, the pointer variable ps can point at objects of both classes, but the pointer variable pgs can only point at objects of type grad_student. We wish to study how different pointer assignments affect the invocation of a version of print. The first instance of the statement

```
ps -> print();
```

invokes student::print. It is pointing at the variable s1 of type student. The multiple assignment statement

```
ps = pgs = &gs1;
```

has both pointers pointing at an object of type grad_student. The assignment to ps involves an implicit conversion. The second instance of the statement

```
ps -> print();
```

again invokes student::print. The fact that this pointer is pointing at a grad_student variable gs1 is not relevant. The statement

```
pgs -> print();      //grad_student::print
```

invokes grad_student::print. The variable pgs is of type pointer to grad_student and when invoked with an object of this type selects a member function from this class.

6.5. Virtual Functions

Overloaded member functions are selected to be invoked by a type matching algorithm that includes having the implicit argument matched to an object of that class type. All of this is known at compile-time and allows the compiler to select the appropriate member directly. As will become apparent, it would be nice to dynamically select at run-time the appropriate member function from among basc and dcrived class functions. The keyword `virtual` is a function specifier that provides such a mechanism, but it may be used only to modify member function declarations.

A `virtual` function must be executable code. When invoked, its semantics are the same as other functions. In a derived class, its name can be overloaded and the function prototype of the derived function must have matching type. The selection of which function to invoke from among a group of overloaded `virtual` functions is dynamic. The typical case is where a base class has a virtual function and derived classes have their versions of this function. A pointer to base class can point at either a base class object or a derived class object. The member function selected will depend on the class of the object being pointed at, not on the pointer type. In the absence of a derived type member, the base class virtual function is used by default.

Consider the following example:

```
//virtual function selection
#include <stream.h>

class B {
public:
    int  i;
    virtual void print_i() { cout << i << " inside B\n"; }
};

class D1 : public B {
public:
    void print_i() { cout << i << " inside D1\n"; }
};

class D2 : private B {
public:
    int i;
    D2() { B::i = 4; }
    void print_i() { cout << i << " inside D2 B::i is "
                          << B::i << "\n"; }
};
```

```
main()
{
    B    b;
    B*   pb = &b;
    D1   f;
    D2   h;

    h.i = 1 + (f.i = 1 + (b.i = 1));
    pb -> print_i();
    pb = &f;
    pb -> print_i();
    pb = (B*)&h;
    pb -> print_i();
}
```

The output from this program is

```
1 inside B
2 inside D1
3 inside D2 B::i is 0
```

In each case a different version of print_i is executed. Selection depends dynamically on the object being pointed at. Different class objects are processed by different functions determined at run-time. Facilities that allow the implementation of ADTs, inheritance, and the ability to process objects dynamically are the essentials of OOP.

The last line of output requires some explanation. The derived class D2 has both a private and public variable i. Its private variable was inherited privately from the base class variable i, and it can be accessed by the member function print_i using scope resolution. Because D2 is privately derived, it is not a subtype of B and the cast is required to allow pb to point at h.

Only member functions can be virtual. One last restriction: Constructors cannot be virtual. Destructors can be virtual.

6.6. An Example: A Class Hierarchy

We will further demonstrate object-oriented programming. The stack implementation of Chapter 4 will be modified to store pointers, and a class hierarchy will be used to create various ADTs. In this hierarchy, the base class proc_data is the common ancestor of the derived classes.

Processing of these varied data types will be dynamic because it will involve a virtual function in the base class.

We begin by showing the hierarchy of derived classes.

```
class proc_data {
public:
    virtual void print() { cout << "virtual\n"; }
};

struct X {
    int   age;
    char name[20];
};

class X_data : public proc_data {
    X* d;
public:
    X_data(int i, char* n)
        { d = new X; d -> age = i; strcpy(d -> name, n); }
    ~X_data() { delete d; }
    void print() { cout << form("%20s %d yrs ",
                                d -> name, d -> age); }

};

struct Y {
    int   salary;
    char name[20];
};

class Y_data : public proc_data {
    Y* d;
public:
    Y_data(int i, char* n)
        { d = new Y; d -> salary = i; strcpy(d -> name, n); }
    ~Y_data() { delete d; }
    void print() { cout << form("%20s $%d ",
                                d -> name, d -> salary); }

};

struct Z {
    int   phone;
    char state[5];
};
```

```
class Z_data : public Y_data {
   Z* z;
public:
   Z_data(int i, char* n, int ph, char* st):Y_data(i, n)
      { z = new Z; z -> phone = ph; strcpy(z -> state, st); }
   ~Z_data() {delete z; }
   void print()
   {
      Y_data::print();
      cout << form("%9d ph %5s\n", z -> phone, z -> state);
   }
};
```

The root of this class hierarchy is `proc_data`, which can be used to hold a variety of virtual functions that will be used to process the objects derived from it. This feature leads to a high degree of code sharing and encapsulation. Each class is separately responsible for defining its functionality, and each class can employ routines from an ancestor class.

Type hierarchy with base class proc_data

■ DISSECTION OF THE *proc_data* CLASSES

```
class proc_data {
public:
   virtual void print() { cout << "virtual\n"; }
};
```

● This class will house all of the virtual and default functions. Sometimes, as is the case here, the virtual function is only for diagnostic purposes.

```
struct X {
    int   age;
    char name[20];
};

class X_data : public proc_data {
    X* d;
public:
    X_data(int i, char* n)
        { d = new X; d -> age = i; strcpy(d -> name, n); }
    ~X_data() { delete d; }
    void print() { cout << form("%20s %d yrs ",
                                    d -> name, d -> age); }
};
```

● The derived class X_data manipulates pointers to type struct X. A record-keeping system could be gradually developed that implemented a variety of such types that could be used to contain, access, and operate on different structure types. Our example system will only implement print for these various classes.

```
struct Y {
    . . .
};

class Y_data : public proc_data {
    Y* d;
    . . .
};

struct Z {
    int   phone;
    char state[5];
};
```

```
class Z_data : public Y_data {
   Z* z;
public:
   Z_data(int i, char* n, int ph, char* st):Y_data(i, n)
      { z = new Z; z -> phone = ph; strcpy(z -> state, st); }
   ~Z_data() { delete z; }
   void print()
   {
      Y_data::print();
      cout << form("%9d ph %5s\n", z -> phone, z -> state);
   }
};
```

- Class z_data derives from y_data, which derives from proc_data. The z_data constructor invokes the y_data constructor, building an anonymous object of type struct Y. The overloaded print invokes its parent's member function Y_data::print to process the name and salary information, before printing phone and state information. Similar code sharing can be distributed throughout this class hierarchy for other needed functions.

We modify the stack type to be a stack of pointers of type proc_data*. Using this pointer type will allow any item of information to be manipulated dynamically by an overloaded virtual function.

```
typedef proc_data* p_type;
enum boolean {false, true};

class stack {
   p_type* s;
   int      max_len;
   int      top;
public:
   stack(int size)
      { s = new p_type[size]; max_len = size; top = 0; }
   void    reset() { top = 0; }
   void    push(p_type& c) { top++; s[top] = c; }
   p_type  pop() { return (s[top--]); }
   p_type  top_of() { return (s[top]); }
   boolean empty() { return (top == 0); }
   boolean full() { return (top == max_len - 1); }
};
```

This modification of an existing class required mostly changes from type char to p_type. It is another potent demonstration of the ease in which such a type system is extended.

Let us see how all this works in a simple test.

```
main()
{
    proc_data*  temp[10];
    stack st(10);

    temp[0] = new Y_data(24000, "Sue Hawkins");
    temp[1] = new X_data(18, "Ken Hawkins");
    temp[2] = new Z_data(19990, "Igon Hawkins", 5551110, "CA");

    for (int i = 0; i < 3; ++i)
        st.push(temp[i]);
    for (i = 0; i < 3; ++i) {
        st.pop() -> print();
        cout << "\n";
    }
}
```

The output produced is

```
Igon Hawkins $19990     5551110 ph      CA

Ken Hawkins 18 yrs
Sue Hawkins $24000
```

6.7. A Binary Tree Class

Let us define a generic binary tree class, which will be used to store generic pointers. Since such a class is not very useful, we will derive from it a class that can store useful information.

```
//binary search tree

#include <stream.h>

typedef void    (*pfct)(void*);
typedef void*    p_gen;

class bnode {
    friend  class bstree;
    bnode*  left;
    bnode*  right;
    p_gen   data;
    int     count;
    bnode(p_gen d, bnode* l, bnode* r)
        { data = d; left = l; right = r; count = 1; }
    friend int comp(p_gen a, p_gen b);
    friend void prt(bnode* n);
};

class bstree {
    bnode* root;
public:
    bstree() { root = 0; }
    void insert(p_gen d);
    p_gen find(p_gen d) { return (find(root, d)); }
    p_gen find(bnode* r, p_gen d);
    void apply(pfct f) { traverse(root, f); }
    void traverse(bnode* r, pfct f);
};
```

The individual nodes in this binary tree store a generic pointer data and an int count that will count duplicate entries. The pointer data will match a pointer type in the derived class. The tree will be a binary search tree that will store nodes of smaller value to the left, and larger or equal values to the right. We need a method of comparing values that is appropriate to the specific derived type. We use a friend function comp that is a friend of bnode and will be coded appropriately for the derived class.

The insert function places nodes in a tree, and it must find the position in the tree for the new nodes. The function p_gen(bnode* r, p_gen d) searches the subtree rooted at r, for the information represented by d. The overloaded function p_gen find(p_gen d) searches the entire tree. The member function void traverse(bnode* r, pfct f) walks around the subtree rooted at r, applying the argument function f to each node in turn. This is done for the entire tree by void apply(pfct f).

```
void bstree::insert(p_gen d)
{
    bnode* temp = root;
    bnode* old;

    if (root == 0) {
        root = new bnode(d, 0, 0);
        return;
    }
    while (temp != 0) {
        old = temp;
        if (comp(temp -> data, d) == 0) {
            (temp -> count)++;
            return;
        }
        if (comp(temp -> data, d) > 0)
            temp = temp -> left;
        else
            temp = temp -> right;
    }
    if (comp(old -> data, d) > 0)
        old -> left = new bnode(d, 0, 0);
    else
        old -> right = new bnode(d, 0, 0);
}
```

The insert function creates a one-node tree if the tree is initially empty.
If the information as represented by the pointer d matches existing information as determined by comp, then count is incremented. Otherwise
comp navigates through the tree to the appropriate leaf position, where
the new node is constructed and attached. Note that the function comp
can be computationally expensive, and multiple evaluations of it can be
eliminated (see exercise 16).

```
p_gen bstree::find(bnode* r, p_gen d)
{
    if (r == 0)
        return (0);
    else if (comp(r -> data, d) ==  0)
        return (r -> data);
    else if (comp(r -> data, d) > 0)
        return (find( r -> left, d));
    else
        return (find( r -> right, d));
}
```

This is a standard recursion. If the information as pointed at by d is not found, 0 is returned.

The following is also a standard recursion. At each node the formal argument f is applied.

```
void bstree::traverse(bnode* r, pfct f)
{
    if (r != 0) {
        traverse (r -> left, f);
        (*f)(r);
        traverse (r -> right, f);
    }
}
```

We derive a class capable of storing a pointer to char as its data member.

```
#include "gtree.h"
#include <string.h>

class s_tree : bstree {
public:
    s_tree() {}
    void  insert(char* d) { bstree::insert(p_gen(d)); }
    char* find(char* d)
            { return ((char*)bstree::find(p_gen(d))); }
    void print() { bstree::apply((pfct)prt); }
};
```

The base class insertion function bstree::insert takes a generic pointer type as its argument. The derived class insertion function s_tree::insert takes a pointer to char as its argument. Therefore in the derived class s_tree

```
void  insert(char* d) { bstree::insert(p_gen(d)); }
```

uses the explicit conversion p_gen(d).

We need a function to perform comparison: the promised friend function to class bnode.

```
int comp(p_gen i, p_gen j)
{
    return (strcmp((char*)i, (char*)j));
}
```

We also show how to use the traversal mechanism to provide a print routine for the entire tree. This requires a function of type pfct that is applied at each node.

```
void prt(bnode* n)
{
    cout << (char*)n -> data << "\t" ;
    cout << n -> count << "\t";
}
```

There is a good deal more abstraction in the design of s_tree than would be the case for a like structure written in C. The payback for this is the ease with which further classes that utilize the underlying binary tree structure can be derived.

6.8. Summary

1. Inheritance is the mechanism of *deriving* a new class from an old one. That is, the existing class can be added to or altered to create the derived class. Through inheritance a hierarchy of related ADTs can be created that share code.

2. A class can be derived from an existing class using the form:

> class *class-name* : (public|private) *optional* *base-class-name*
> {
>   *member declarations*
> };

As usual, the keyword class can be replaced by the keyword struct, with the usual implication that members are default public.

3. The keywords public, private, and protected are available as visibility modifiers for class members. A public member is visible throughout its scope. A private member is visible to other member functions within its own class. A protected member is visible to other member functions within its class and any class immediately derived from it. These visibility modifiers can be used within a class declaration in any order and with any frequency.

4. The derived class has its own constructors, which will invoke the base class constructor. There is a special syntax to pass arguments from the derived class constructor back to the base class constructor.

   function header : *base-class-name* _{*optional*} *(argument list)*

5. A publicly derived class is a *subtype* of its base class. A variable of the derived class can in many ways be treated as if it were the base class type. A pointer whose type is pointer to base class can point to objects of the publicly derived class type.

6. A reference to the derived class may be implicitly converted to a reference to the public base class. It is possible to declare a reference to a base class and initialize it to a reference to an object of the publicly derived class.

7. The keyword `virtual` is a function specifier that provides a mechanism to dynamically select at run-time the appropriate member function from among base and derived class functions. It may be used only to modify member function declarations.

8. Facilities that allow the implementation of ADTs, inheritance, and the ability to process objects dynamically are the essentials of OOP.

6.9. Exercises

1. Change the declaration of `grad_student` found in Section 6.1 to

```
class grad_student : student {
public:
    enum {ta, ra, fellowship, other} support;
    char dept[10];
    char thesis[80];
    void print();
};
```

Explain what goes wrong in the following code:

```
main()
{
    grad_student s;

    strcpy(s.name, "Charles Babbage");
    . . .
}
```

Does this work if the default `private` derivation is changed to an explicit `protected` derivation?

2. The safe array member `vect_bnd::operator[]` in Section 6.3 is guaranteed to be passed a properly indexed element in the `return` statement

```
return (vect::operator[] (i - l_bnd));
```

This means that the array index is unnecessarily checked twice. Add an unchecked access function as a member function of `class vect`

```
int& elem(int i);    //unchecked indexing
```

Use this to modify the `return` statement so as not to recheck the index.

3. Write a member function `print()` that prints out a variable of type `vect_bnd`.

4. Write two new constructors for `vect_bnd`:

```
//initialize by vect_bnd
vect_bnd::vect_bnd(vect_bnd& v);

//initialize by array
vect_bnd::vect_bnd(int a[], int l, int u);
```

5. Develop a type `matrix_bnd`

```
class matrix_bnd : public matrix {
    int lb1, lb2, ub1, ub2;
    int size1, size2;
public:
    matrix_bnd(matrix_bnd& m); //copy existing matrix
    matrix_bnd();                   //5 × 5 matrix
    matrix_bnd(int l1, int u1, int l2, int u2);
    void print();
    . . .
};
```

In OOP, objects should know how to print themselves, and we have frequently made `print` a member function of a class. Notationally, it is also useful to overload << for user-defined ADTs. In this chapter we develop output functions for `card` and `deck` that illustrate these techniques.

7.1. The Output Class `ostream`

Output is returned to an object of type `ostream` as described in *stream.h*. An operator << is overloaded in this class to perform output conversions from standard types. The operator is left associative and returns a value of type `ostream&`. The standard output `ostream` corresponding to `stdout` is `cout` and the standard output `ostream` corresponding to `stderr` is `cerr`.

The effect of executing a simple output statement such as

```
cout << "x = " << x << "\n";
```

is to print to the screen first a string of four characters followed by an appropriate representation for the output of x followed by a new line. The representation depends on which overloaded version of << is invoked. For example, on some systems if x is of type `char`, its integer representation is printed. This is because type `char` is converted to `int` and << is not explicitly overloaded with `char` as an argument type. It is also the case that on some systems the overloading mechanism does not discriminate between `char` and `int`.

The class `ostream` contains public members such as

```
ostream& operator<<(int i);
ostream& operator<<(long i);
ostream& operator<<(double x);
ostream& operator<<(char* s);
ostream& put(char c);
```

The member function `put` outputs the character representation of `c`. Since this is an ordinary member function, it would be used as follows:

```
c = 'A';
cout.put('B');       //output B
cout.put(99);        //output c   ascii value 99
cout.put(c + 3);     //output D
```

7.2. Formatted Output `form()`

As given, the *put to* operator << does not produce formatted output. A typical program error is seen in the following:

```
int  i = 8, j = 9;
cout << i << j ;           //prints 89
cout << i << "    " << j;  //prints 8    9
```

It is inconvenient to always be inserting padding space explicitly when needed. So, to remedy this, *stream.h* imports six functions that perform formatting. These return a char* to the generated output string, and this string gets explicitly printed by <<.

---

format functions

char* dec(long d, int width = 0);	decimal
char* oct(long o, int width = 0);	octal
char* hex(long x, int width = 0);	hexadecimal
char* chr(int c, int width = 0);	character
char* str(char* s, int width = 0);	string
char* form(const char*, ...);	general facility

The first five functions print an appropriate string of length width. It is right justified and padded on the left with blanks. If the width is omitted, the default value 0 produces a string that is exactly the width of the output representation without blanks.

The form function has two nice properties that allow flexible use at a high level. First, a list of arguments of arbitrary length can be printed, and second, the printing is controlled by simple formats. This is analogous to the printf function in *stdio.h*. The argument list to form has two parts:

control_string   and   *other arguments*

In the example

```
form("%d / %f =  %f", 9, 3.3, 9 / 3.3);
```

we have

$$control\_string:\quad \texttt{"\%d / \%f = \%f"}$$
$$other\_arguments:\quad \texttt{9, 3.3, 9 / 3.3}$$

The expressions in *other_arguments* are evaluated and converted according to the formats in the control string, and then placed in the output stream. Characters in the control string that are not part of a format are placed directly in the output stream. The % symbol introduces a format, or conversion specification. A single conversion specification is a string that begins with % and ends with a conversion character. The conversion characters and other formatting commands are the same as those used in C by `printf`. We review them here.

Conversion character	How the corresponding argument is printed
c	character
d	decimal integer
i	decimal integer
u	unsigned decimal integer
o	unsigned octal integer
x	unsigned hexadecimal integer
X	unsigned hexadecimal integer
e	floating point number; example: 6.310000e+01
E	floating point number; example: 6.310000E+01
f	floating point number; example: 63.10000
g	e-format or f-format, whichever is shorter
G	E-format or f-format, whichever is shorter
s	string
p	pointer in hexadecimal

Explicit formatting information may be included in a conversion specification. If it is not included, then certain defaults occur. For example, the format %f is printed with six digits to the right of the decimal point by default. Explicit formatting information is specified as follows. Between the % sign and the conversion character there may be

- a minus sign, which means that the converted argument is to be *left adjusted* in its field. If there is no minus sign, then the converted argument is to be *right adjusted* in its field. The place where an argument is printed is called its *field*, and the number of spaces used to print an argument is called its *field width*.

- a plus sign, which means that a nonnegative number is to have a + prepended. This works with the conversion characters d, i, e, E, f, g, and G. All negative numbers automatically have a − prepended.

- a blank instead of a plus sign, which means that a nonnegative number is to have a blank prepended. This works with the conversion characters d, i, e, E, f, g, and G.

- a #, which has a meaning that depends on the conversion character. In an o-format it causes 0 to be prepended to the octal number being printed. In an x- or x-format it causes 0x or 0x to be prepended to the hexadecimal number being printed. In a g- or G-format it causes trailing zeros to be printed. In an e-, E-, f-, g-, or G-format, it causes a decimal point to be printed, even with precision 0.

- a positive integer, which defines the *field width* of the converted argument. If the converted argument has fewer characters than the specified field width, then it will be padded with blanks on the left or right, depending on whether the converted argument is right or left adjusted. If the converted argument has more characters than the specified field width, then the field width will be extended to "whatever is required." If the integer defining the field width begins with 0, and the argument being printed is right adjusted in its field, then 0s rather than blanks will be used for padding.

- a period, which separates *field width* from *precision*.

- a nonnegative integer, which defines the *precision* of the converted argument. For an e, E, f, g, or G conversion this is the number of digits to the right of the decimal point. For an s conversion it is the maximum number of characters to be printed from a string.

- the character 1, which specifies that the conversion character d, i, o, x, or u that follows corresponds to an argument of type long or that the conversion character e, E, f, g, or G that follows corresponds to an argument of type double. Similarly, the character h specifies that the conversion character d, i, o, x, or u that follows corresponds to an argument of type short.

- a *, which indicates that a value is to be obtained from the argument list. The field width or precision or both may be indicated by a * instead of by a nonnegative integer.

The field width is the minimum number of spaces that must be used to print the expression. The default is whatever is required to properly display the argument. Thus the integer value 102 (decimal) will require three spaces for decimal conversion d or octal conversion o, but only two spaces for hexadecimal conversion x. These digits will appear right adjusted unless the minus sign is present. If the field width is too short to properly display the value of the corresponding argument, the field width will be increased to the default. If the entire field is not needed to display the converted argument, then the remaining part of the field is padded with blanks on the left or right, depending on whether the converted argument is right or left adjusted. The padding character on the left can be made o by specifying the field width with a leading zero.

The precision is specified by a nonnegative number that occurs to the right of the period. For string conversions this is the maximum number of characters to be printed from the string. For floating point conversions this is the number of digits to be printed to the right of the decimal point. Examples of formats are given in the table that follows. We use double quote characters to visually delimit the field. They are not part of what gets printed.

Declarations and initializations			
char	c = 'w';		
int	i = 1, j = 29;		
float	x = 333.12345678901234567890;		
double	y = 333.12345678901234567890;		
char	s1[] = "she sells sea shells";		
Format	Expression	How it is printed in its field	Remarks
%c	c	"w"	field length 1 by default
%2c	c	" w"	right adjusted
%-3c	c	"w "	left adjusted
%d	-j	"-29"	field length 3 by default
%010d	i	"0000000001"	padded with zeros
%-12d	j	"29 "	left adjusted
%12o	j	" 35"	octal, right adjusted
%-12x	j	"1d "	hexadecimal, left adjusted
%f	x	"333.123444"	precision 6 by default
%.1f	x	"333.1"	precision 1
%20.3f	x	" 333.123"	right adjusted
%-20.3e	y	"3.331e+002 "	left adjusted
%s	s1	"she sells sea shells"	field length 20 by default
%7s	s1	"she sells sea shells"	more space needed

To print the character % in the output stream one can use the conversion specification %%, which prints a single percent symbol. Of course, the conversion specification %c can be used to print the expression '%' in the argument list.

7.3. User-Defined Types: Output

User-defined types have been printed by typically creating a member function print. Let us use the types card and deck of Section 3.9 as an example of a simple user-defined type. We write out a set of output routines for displaying cards.

```
//card output

#include  <stream.h>

char pips_symbol[14] = { '?', 'A', '2', '3', '4', '5', '6',
                         '7', '8', '9', 'T', 'J', 'Q', 'K'};
char suit_symbol[4] = { 'c', 'd', 'h', 's'};

enum suit {clubs, diamonds, hearts, spades};

class pips {
   int  p;
public:
   void assign(int n) { p = n % 13 + 1; }
   void print() { cout << chr(pips_symbol[p], 2); }
};

class card {
   int  cd;           //a cd is from 0 to 51
public:
   suit s;
   pips p;
   void assign(int n) { cd = n; s = n / 13; p.assign(n); }
   void pr_card() { p.print(); cout << chr(suit_symbol[s]); }
};

class deck {
   card d[52];
public:
   void init_deck();
   void shuffle();
   void deal(int, int, card*);
   void pr_deck();
};

void deck::pr_deck()
{
   for (int i = 0; i < 52; ++i) {
      if (i % 13 == 0)        //13 cards to a line
         cout << "\n";
      d[i].pr_card();
   }
}
```

In this solution we use the format function chr. Each card will be printed out in three characters. If d is a variable of type deck, then d. pr_deck () will print out the entire deck, 13 cards to a line.

In keeping with the spirit of OOP, it would also be nice to overload << to accomplish the same aims. The operator << has two arguments, an ostream and the ADT, and it must produce an ostream. Let us write these functions for the types card and deck.

```
ostream& operator<<(ostream& out, pips x)
{
    return (out << chr(pips_symbol[x.p], 2));
}

ostream& operator<<(ostream& out, card cd)
{
    return (out << cd.p << chr(suit_symbol[cd.s]));
}

ostream& operator<<(ostream& out, deck x)
{
    for (int i = 0; i < 52; ++i) {
        if (i % 13 == 0)            //13 cards to a line
            out << "\n";
        out << x.d[i];
    }
    return (out);
}
```

The functions that operate on pips and deck need to be friends of the corresponding class because they access private members.

A second solution for providing user-defined output for ostreams is to convert a representation of the object to char*, which can be used as is with <<. This solution typically uses form.

```
#include  <string.h>

char* pips::ostring(char* f)
{
    return (form(f, pips_symbol[p]));
}
```

```
//find position of 2nd c in string s
int arg1(char* s, char c)
{
   int  i = 0, cnt = 0;

   while ((cnt += (*s++ == c)) < 2)
      i++;
   return (i);
}

char* card::ostring(char* f)
{
   char f1[40], f2[40];
   int i;

   strncpy(f1, f, i = arg1(f, '%'));
   strcpy(f2, f + i);
   return (strcat(p.ostring(f1), form(f2, suit_symbol[s])));
}

void deck::pr_deck()
{
   for (int i = 0; i < 52; ++i) {
      if (i % 13 == 0)           //13 cards to a line
         cout << "\n";
      cout << d[i].ostring("%2c%c");
   }
}
```

What is interesting here is that a card is printed out by a user-defined format. The format string "%2c%c" is passed to card::ostring, where it is converted into two separate strings f1 and f2. The first format is used by pips::ostring and the second by form. In this code, pips are printed in a two-character width field and suit in a single-character width.

7.4. The Input Class istream

Input is returned to an object of type istream as described in *stream.h*. An operator >> is overloaded in this class to perform input conversions to standard types. The standard input istream corresponding to stdin is cin.

The effect of executing a simple input statement such as

```
cin >> x >> i;
```

is to read from standard input, normally the keyboard, a value for x and then a value for i. White space is ignored.

The class istream contains public members such as

```
istream& operator>>(int& i);
istream& operator>>(long& i);
istream& operator>>(double& x);
istream& operator>>(char& c);
istream& operator>>(char* s);
istream& get(char& c);
istream& get(char* s, int n, int c = '\n');
```

The member function get(char& c) inputs, white space characters included, the character representation to c. The member function get(char* s, int n, int c = '\n') inputs into the string pointed at by s at most n characters, white space characters included. The optionally specified default character acts as a terminator. If not specified, the input is read up to the next newline. Since this is an ordinary member function it would be used as follows:

```
cin.get(c);            //one character
cin.get(s, 40);        //length 40 or terminated by '\n'
cin.get(s, 10, '*');   //length 10 or terminated by *
```

When overloading the operator >> to produce input to a user-defined type, the typical form of such a function prototype is:

```
istream& operator>>(istream& p, user-defined type& x)
```

If the function needs access to private members of x, it must be made a friend of its class. A key point is to make x a reference parameter so its value can be modified.

7.5. Files

C systems have stdin, stdout, and stderr as standard files. In addition, systems may define other standard files, such as stdprn and stdaux. Abstractly, a file may be thought of as a stream of characters that are processed sequentially.

Written in C	Name	Remark
stdin	standard input file	connected to the keyboard
stdout	standard output file	connected to the screen
stderr	standard error file	connected to the screen
stdprn	standard printer file	connected to the printer
stdaux	standard auxiliary file	connected to an auxiliary port

The C++ stream input/output ties the first three of these standard files to `cin`, `cout`, and `cerr`, respectively. Typically, C++ ties `cprn` and `caux` to their corresponding standard files `stdprn` and `stdaux`. Other files can be opened or created by the programmer. We shall show how to do this in the context of writing a program to double-space an existing file into an existing or new file. The file names will be specified on the command line and passed in to `argv`.

The `class ostream` and the `class istream` both have constructors. One such constructor, `ostream::ostream(streambuf* s)`, allows a buffer to be associated with a stream. The `class filebuf` is a special case of `streambuf` used by files. To properly open and manage an `istream` or `ostream` related to a system file, you

1. Declare a `filebuf`.

2. Open the corresponding file for input or output.

3. Call a constructor with the address of the `filebuf`.

The function `filebuf::filebuf* open(char*, open_mode)` is used to open the file named in the first argument. The second argument is an enumerated type

```
enum open_mode {input, output, append};
```

and specifies what mode is required. If file opening fails, the value 0 is returned.

```
//dbl_sp: a program to double space a file
//Usage: executable  f1 f2
//f1 must be present and readable
//f2 must be writable if it exists

#include <stream.h>

main(int argc, char** argv)
{
    void        double_space(istream&, ostream&);
    filebuf    f_in, f_out;

    if (argc != 3) {
        cout << "\nUsage: " << argv[0]
             << "  infile  outfile\n";
        exit(1);
    }
    if (!f_in.open(argv[1], input)) {
        cerr << "cannot open " << argv[1];
        exit(1);
    }
    istream  in(&f_in);
    if (!f_out.open(argv[2], output)) {
        cerr << "cannot open " << argv[2];
        exit(1);
    }
    ostream  out(&f_out);
    double_space(in, out);
}

void double_space(istream& f, ostream& t)
{
    char   c;

    while (f.get(c)) {
        t.put(c);
        if (c == '\n')
            t.put(c);
    }
}
```

■ DISSECTION OF THE *dbl_sp* PROGRAM

```
filebuf    f_in, f_out;
```

- The variable f_in is used for input and the variable f_out is used for output. They are used to create corresponding istream and ostream variables.

```
if  (!f_in.open(argv[1], input)) {
   cerr << "cannot open " << argv[1];
   exit(1);
}
istream   in(&f_in);
```

- The member function open is invoked to open for input the command line argument argv[1], which names the input file. If this fails—for example, if the file does not exist or is unreadable—then an error exit is executed. If opening succeeds, the istream in is constructed connected to the filebuf f_in. At this point f_in can be used analogously to cin.

```
if  (!f_out.open(argv[2], output)) {
   cerr << "cannot open " << argv[2];
   exit(1);
}
ostream   out(&f_out);
```

- The file named in argv[2] is either opened for writing or is created with write permission. If opening succeeds, the ostream out is constructed connected to the filebuf f_out. At this point f_out can be used analogously to cout.

```
double_space(in, out);
```

- The actual double spacing from the input file to the output file occurs here.

```
void double_space(istream& f, ostream& t)
{
    char  c;

    while (f.get(c)) {
        t.put(c);
        if (c == '\n')
            t.put(c);
    }
}
```

- The `get` member function gets a character from an `istream`.
  The `put` member function puts a character to an `ostream`.
  The newline character is outputted twice, creating the desired
  double spacing in the output file.

7.6. The Functions and Macros in *ctype.h*

The system provides a standard header file *ctype.h*, which contains a set
of macros that are used to test characters and a set of functions that are
used to convert characters. This is a standard C header file but is mentioned here because of its usefulness in C++ input/output. Those macros
that only test a character return an `int` value that is nonzero (*true*) or 0
(*false*). The argument is type `int`.

Macro	Nonzero (true) is returned if:
`isalpha(c)`	c is a letter
`isupper(c)`	c is an uppercase letter
`islower(c)`	c is a lowercase letter
`isdigit(c)`	c is a digit
`isxdigit(c)`	c is a hexadecimal digit
`isspace(c)`	c is a white space character
`isalnum(c)`	c is a letter or digit
`ispunct(c)`	c is a punctuation character
`isprint(c)`	c is a printable character
`iscntrl(c)`	c is a control character
`isascii(c)`	c is an ASCII code

Other functions provide for the appropriate conversion of a character value. Note carefully that these functions do not change the value of c stored in memory.

Function	Effect
toupper(c)	changes c from lowercase to uppercase
tolower(c)	changes c from uppercase to lowercase
toascii(c)	changes c to ASCII code

7.7. Using Stream States

Each istream or ostream has an associated state that can be tested. The states are as follows:

```
enum stream_state {_good, _eof, _fail, _bad};
```

This value is held in the private member variable state. The values for a particular stream can be tested using the overloaded public member function rdstate. The state can also be tested by using member functions good, eof, fail, and bad to test these conditions separately.

Applying input/output operations to streams not in the state _good leads to a null operation, and can cause a program to hang up. The member function clear can reset a stream to _good.

A stream state of _good means the previous input/output operation worked and the next operation should succeed. A stream state of _eof means the previous input operation returned an end-of-file condition. A stream state of _fail means the previous input/output operation failed but did not lose any characters in the stream. And a stream state of _bad means the previous input/output operation failed but may have lost some characters in the stream.

The following program counts the number of words coming from the standard input. Normally this would be redirected to use an existing file. It illustrates ideas discussed in this and the last two sections.

```
//A word count program
//Usage: executable < file
#include    <stream.h>
#include    <ctype.h>

main()
{
    int    word_cnt = -1;
    void   found_next_word(void);

    while (cin.good()) {
        ++word_cnt;
        found_next_word();
    }
    cout << "word count is " << word_cnt << "\n";
}

void found_next_word(void)
{
    char    c;

    cin >> c;
    while (!isspace(c))
        cin.get(c);
}
```

■ DISSECTION OF THE *word_cnt* PROGRAM

```
int    word_cnt = -1;
```

- The int variable word_cnt is initialized to −1. The program
  will count one extra before detecting an end-of-file condition.

```
while (cin.good()) {
    ++word_cnt;
    found_next_word();
}
```

- As long as the input stream state associated with cin is
  _good, the body of the while loop is executed, causing

word_cnt to be incremented. The function found_next_word attempts to read the next word.

```
void found_next_word(void)
{
    char    c;

    cin >> c;
    while (!isspace(c))
        cin.get(c);
}
```

- A non–white space character is gotten from the input stream and assigned to c. The while loop tests that adjacent characters are not white space. The loop terminates when a white space character is found, because this indicates that a word has been found. If the function encounters an end-of-file, it sets the stream state for cin and causes cin.good() in main to terminate its while loop. One last point: The loop cannot be rewritten

```
    while (!isspace(c))
        cin >> c;
```

because this would skip white space.

7.8. Summary

1. C++ introduces *stream.h*, which implements a wide range of input/output functions, many of which overload the operators << and >>.

2. Output is returned to an object of type ostream. An operator << is overloaded in this class to perform output conversions from standard types. The standard output ostream corresponding to stdout is cout and the standard output ostream corresponding to stderr is cerr.

3. Formatted output is produced by using one of six standard functions: dec, oct, hex, chr, str, and form. They all return strings with the appropriate output representation.

4. The function `char* form(const char*, ...);` has two nice properties that allow flexible use at a high level. First, a list of arguments
of arbitrary length can be printed, and second, the printing is controlled by simple formats. The argument list to `form` has two parts:

   control_string   and   *other_arguments*

It acts analogously to `printf` in C.

5. One can overload `<<` to output user-defined types. The operator `<<`
has two arguments: an `ostream` and the user-defined type. It must
produce an `ostream`. A typical function that does this is

```
ostream& operator<<(ostream& out, user-defined type x)
{
    return (out << form(. . .));
}
```

6. C systems have `stdin`, `stdout`, and `stderr` as standard files. In
addition, systems may define other standard files, such as `stdprn`
and `stdaux`. Abstractly, a file may be thought of as a stream of
characters that are processed sequentially. The standard files are
defined in *stdio.h*. The C++ stream input/output ties the first three
of these standard files to `cin`, `cout`, and `cerr`, respectively. C++
ties `cprn` and `caux` to their corresponding standard files `stdprn` and
`stdaux`. Other files can be opened or created by the programmer.

7. To properly open and manage an `istream` or `ostream` related to a
system file, you

   Declare a `filebuf`.

   Open the corresponding file for input or output.

   Call a constructor with the address of the `filebuf`.

8. The function `filebuf::filebuf* open(char*, open_mode)` is used to
open the file named in the first argument. The second argument is
an enumerated type

```
enum open_mode {input, output, append};
```

and specifies what mode is required. If file opening fails, the value
0 is returned.

9. Input is returned to an object of type istream as described in *stream.h*. An operator >> is overloaded in this class to perform input conversions to standard types. The standard input istream corresponding to stdin is cin.

10. Each istream or ostream has an associated state that can be tested. The states are as follows:

```
enum stream_state {_good, _eof, _fail, _bad};
```

This value is held in the private member variable state. The values for a particular stream can be tested using the overloaded public member function rdstate. The state can also be tested by using member functions good, eof, fail, and bad to test these conditions separately.

7.9. Exercises

1. Experiment with your system by defining the following:

```
const double e = 2.718281828459045235360287471352;
```

Now print this out using:

```
cout << e;
cout << float(e);
cout << form("%f : %g : %25.20fl : %25.20\n", e, e, e, e);
```

Remember that floating point precision cannot be exact.

2. See if float and double are stored differently on your machine by repeating the above experiment with e declared as float.

3. Use the format functions dec, oct, hex, and chr to write out a table that displays 0–255 in each of these representations. Print each value in a field six characters wide. Some sample output follows from our system:

dec	oct	hex	chr
0	0	0	
1	1	1	.
2	2	2	
. . .			
32	40	20	
33	41	21	!
34	42	22	"
. . .			
65	101	41	A
66	102	42	B
67	103	43	C
. . .			
253	375	fd	
254	376	fe	
255	377	ff	

Explain why the `chr` column does not always print.

4. Exercises 4–6 use the `class clock` from Section 5.6. Overload `<<` to print a standard representation of a `clock` value. Its function prototype should be a friend function of `clock`:

```
friend ostream& operator<<(ostream& out, clock x);
```

5. Write a `clock` member function to produce a string as an output representation of `clock` based on a format. Its prototype is

```
char* ostring(char* f);
```

The format string `f` should be broken into four integer formats to be used to format the four data members `secs`, `mins`, `hours`, and `days`.

6. Overload `>>` to read a standard representation of a `clock` value. Its function prototype should be a friend function of `clock`:

```
friend istream& operator>>(istream& in, clock& x);
```

7. Use the `class complex` from Section 5.3. Overload both `<<` and `>>` to work with `complex` values.

8. Rewrite the *dbl_sp* program so that it gets the name of the input file as a command line argument and writes to `cout`. After this has been done, the command

   dbl_sp infile > outfile

   can be used to double-space whatever is in *infile*, with the output being written into *outfile*.

9. Rewrite the *dbl_sp* program so that it uses a command line option of the form − *n*, where *n* can be 1, 2, or 3. If *n* is 1, then the output should be single-spaced. That is, two or more contiguous newline characters in the input file should be written as a single newline character in the output file. If *n* is 2, then the output file should be strictly double-spaced. That is, one or more contiguous newline characters in the input file should be rewritten as a pair of newline characters in the output file. If *n* is 3, the output file should be strictly triple-spaced. Note, some systems use \r\n (carriage return, newline) to terminate lines.

10. Write a program to number the lines in a file. The input file name should be passed to the program as a command line argument. The program should write to `cout`. Each line in the input file should be written to the output file, with the line number and a space prepended.

11. Read about the system function `unlink()`, on page 320 of *A Book on C* by Al Kelley and Ira Pohl (Benjamin/Cummings, Menlo Park, Calif., 1984). The following program uses this function to remove a file. It is a simple version of the MS-DOS command *del*, which is used to remove files. Modify the program to remove one or more files obtained as command line arguments.

    ```
    main(int argc,char** argv)
    {
        unlink(argv[1]);
    }
    ```

12. The `istream` member function `istream& putback(char c)` is used to push one character back into the stream. Write a program to test this. Can you describe a situation where this would be useful?

13. Write a program that displays a file on the screen 20 lines at a time, with a maximum length of 80 characters per line. The input file should be given as a command line argument. The program should display the next 20 lines after a carriage return has been typed.

14. Modify the previous exercise to display one or more files given as command line arguments. Also, allow a command line option of the form $-n$ to be used, where n is a positive integer specifying the number of lines that are to be displayed at one time.

15. Since cout and cerr are both an ostream, what is the effect of the assignment

```
cerr = cout;
```

Advanced Features

This chapter describes some advanced features of C++ and recent additions to the language. Most of these changes are described in *The Evolution of C++: 1985 to 1987* by Bjarne Stroustrup (USENIX C++ Papers, Santa Fe, N.M., 1987, pp. 1–21). These changes are incorporated into the AT&T version 2.0 compiler.

Chief among these advanced features is multiple inheritance, which allows a derived class to include inherited members from more than one ancestor class. A second important change is that default assignment and initialization is no longer bitwise copy. These and other advanced topics will be discussed.

8.1. Multiple Inheritance

The examples in the text thus far require only single inheritance; that is, they require that a class is derived from a single base class. This feature can lead to a chain of derivations wherein class B is derived from class A and class C is derived from class B, . . ., and class N is derived from class M. In effect, N ends up being based on A, B, . . ., M. This chain must not be circular, however, so a class cannot have itself as an ancestor.

Multiple inheritance allows a derived class to be derived from more than one base class. The syntax of class headers is extended to allow a list of base classes and their privacy designation. An example is

```
class tools {
   . . .

};

class parts {
   . . .

};

class labor {
   . . .

};

class plans : public tools, public parts, public labor {
   . . .

};
```

In this example the derived class plans publicly inherits the members of all three base classes. This parental relationship is described by the inheritance *directed acyclic graph* (DAG). The DAG is a graph structure whose nodes are classes and whose directed edges point from base to derived class. To be legal it cannot be circular, so no class may, through its inheritance chain, inherit from itself.

In deriving an identically named member from different classes, ambiguities may arise. These derivations are allowed provided the user does not make an ambiguous reference to such a member. For example,

```
class tools {
public:
    int cost();
    . . .
};

class labor {
public:
    int cost();
    . . .
};

class parts {
public:
    int cost();
    . . .
};

class plans : public tools, public parts, public labor {
public:
    int tot_cost() { return (parts::cost() + labor::cost()); }
    . . .
};

int foo()
{
    int   price;
    plans* ptr;

    price = ptr -> cost();
    . . .
}
```

In the body of foo the reference to cost is inherently ambiguous. It can be resolved by either properly qualifying cost using the scope resolution operator or adding a member cost to the derived class plans.

One further modification to the original inheritance scheme has been made: virtual inheritance. With multiple inheritance, two base classes can be derived themselves from a common ancestor. If both base classes are used in the ordinary way by their derived class, it will have two subobjects of the common ancestor. This duplication, if not desirable, can be eliminated by using virtual inheritance. An example is:

```
class under_grad : public virtual student {
    . . .

};

class grad : public virtual student {
    . . .

};

class department : public under_grad, public grad,
                   public virtual student {
    . . .

};
```

Without the use of `virtual` in this example, `class department` would have objects of `class::under_grad::student` and `class::grad::student`.

The early releases of C++ left unspecified the order of execution for initializing constructors in base and member constructors. Most of the time these constructions were independent of each other and the results were independent of order. With the addition of multiple inheritance, however, it became unnecessarily hazardous to continue this laxness. Thus the current ordering is

1. Explicit reference to base class constructors in the order in which they are listed after the header colon

2. Unmentioned base classes in the order in which they are declared

3. Explicit reference to member class constructors in the order in which they are listed after the header colon

A further improvement is that the class name is used for each base class initializer. The old style of just using a parenthesized argument list that implicitly called the base class constructor is allowed for single inheritance, but is poor style even for that case. Finally, the associated destructors are called in the reverse order from constructor invocation.

Let us illustrate by elaborating on a previous example.

```
class tools {
    . . .
public:
    tools(char*);
    ~tools();
    . . .
};

class parts {
    . . .
public:
    parts(char*);
    ~parts();
    . . .
};

class labor {
    . . .
public:
    labor(int);
    ~labor();
    . . .
};

class plans : public tools, public parts, public labor {
    . . .
    special a;   //member class with constructor
public:
    plans(int m) : labor(m), tools("lathe"), a(m), parts("widget")
        { . . . }
    ~plans();
    . . .
};
```

In this case the member constructor a(m) appears before the base class constructor parts("widget") but by our rules is invoked last. Since its constructor was last, its destructor is invoked first, followed by ~parts, ~tools, ~labor, and ~plans.

Deriving from virtual base classes has several restrictions. The virtual base class cannot have a constructor with arguments and must be called before all other constructors.

8.2. Default Assignment and Other Additions

In Chapter 5 we discussed overloading the assignment operator. If this operator were not overloaded for a particular user type, then assignment between two objects of that type, for early C++ compilers, was bitwise copy. Current systems default to a more sophisticated member-by-member assignment. This rule is recursive until components that are built-in types are assigned in the usual way.

This rule is safer than the original bitwise copy method. In instances where a class, call it A, had a data member of a different class, call it B, and B had assignment overloaded and A did not, there was a possibility of errors if objects of type A were bitwise copy assigned.

The same idea applies to default initializations. The user in most cases need not have a constructor of type X(X&) for class X. The compiler is responsible for providing both assignment and initialization based on the recursive member-by-member subassignment rule. Of course, the user can still overload these member functions to produce a different result where necessary.

A further change allows the operators `new` and `delete` to be overloaded. This feature provides a simple mechanism for user-defined manipulation of free store. Older methods for directly controlling allocation involved the explicit manipulation of the `this` pointer, as described in Section 4.8. We modify that example as follows:

```
class X {
  . . .
public:
    void* operator new(unsigned size) { return (malloc(size)); }
    void  operator delete(X* ptr) { free((void*)ptr); }
    X(unsigned size) { new(size); }
    ~X() { delete(this); }
  . . .
};
```

Other technical changes include the ability to overload the operator ->, distinguishing between signed and unsigned by the overloading selection algorithm, and the use of the scope resolution operator to define pointer to member types. For more details, the reader is directed to the previously cited Stroustrup paper, *The Evolution of C++ : 1985 to 1987*.

8.3. Standard *.h Files

We have made extensive use of *stream.h*, the standard system header
file describing available stream I/O declarations, operations, and functions. However, the C++ system frequently provides other useful libraries that are accessible by including their corresponding *.h* files.

The standard practice on UNIX systems is to place standard *.h* files
in the directory *usr/include/CC*. Among these standard files are *com-
plex.h*, *vector.h*, *nlist.h*, and *assert.h*. Many of the files describe system-
provided classes. An example would be *complex.h*, which provides a
complex number data type. As C++ becomes more widespread one can
expect an increase in the number of such available system-provided types.

The *limits.h* file is particularly important when writing portable
software. It contains macros that define system-dependent values. For
example, *limits.h* is similar to the following:

```
/* Implementation limits */

#ifndef LIMITS_H
#define LIMITS_H        1

#define      CHAR_BIT       8
#define      CHAR_MAX       127
#define      CHAR_MIN       0
#define      SCHAR_MAX      127
#define      SCHAR_MIN      (-128)
#define      UCHAR_MAX      255

       . . .

#define      DBL_RADIX      2
#define      DBL_ROUNDS     1
#define      DBL_MAX_EXP    308
#define      DBL_MIN_EXP    (-307)
#define      DBL_DIG        15

#define      FLT_RADIX      2
#define      FLT_ROUNDS     1
#define      FLT_MAX_EXP    38
#define      FLT_MIN_EXP    (-37)
#define      FLT_DIG        6

#define      LDBL_RADIX     DBL_RADIX
       . . .

#endif /* LIMITS_H */
```

This file is written with C style comments since it must be used by both the ANSI C and C++ compilers, and its values are typical for IBM personal computers. One can see that `long double` is the same as `double`. Code that must be portable and is sensitive to these parameters should be written using these mnemonic constants.

The *assert.h* file supports an assertion macro that is very useful for source-level debugging. Its form is

```
assert(expression);
```

and if the *expression* evaluates to 0, meaning false, the program terminates with an error indication that includes the file name and source line of the failure. A trivial example is:

```
//Using assert.h to check for bugs

#include <stream.h>
#include <assert.h>

main()
{
    int i = 7, j = 5;

    assert(i < j);
}
```

The output is in `stderr` and reads as follows:

```
Assertion failed: file "assert.c", line 10
```

where *assert.c* is the source file.

8.4. External Linkage

Large C programs are partitioned into multifile units that can be compiled separately. Linking such separate modules requires resolving external references. In C the rules for resolving external references are frequently system-dependent.

In C++ these rules are explicit. The key difference is that external nonstatic variables must be defined in exactly one place. As usual, `static extern` constructs can be defined in multiple files because they are local to a given file. Use of the keyword `extern` together with an initializer constitutes defining a variable. Using the keyword `extern` without an initializer constitutes a declaration but not a definition. The following examples illustrate these rules. The first example is legal.

```
//file prog1.c
    char   c;              //definition of c
    . . .

//file prog2.c
    extern char c;         //declaration of c
    . . .
```

The second example is illegal.

```
//file prog1.c
    char    c;
    double x = 0.9;
    . . .

//file prog2.c
    char            c;        //illegal second definition
    extern int      x;        //illegal type mismatch
    extern int      k;        //illegal no declaration
    . . .
```

These two files have three errors. Most C compilers would only complain about the type mismatch. The third error has the variable `k` defined, but not declared.

Constant definitions and `inline` definitions can be duplicated. In general, it is good style to avoid reliance on the `#define` mechanism to produce simple constants and macros. Macro expansion occurs as string replacement and leads to subtle errors in the source code. One can also duplicate type definitions, function declarations, and enumerations. For particular applications, it is desirable to place related definitions into header files. Good examples of this are found in the system header files, such as *stream.h*.

8.5. Iterators

Iterators were mentioned briefly in exercises 5.10 and 5.11. An iterator is a mechanism for accessing all components of a given type. The `for` statement provides a built-in iterator for simple arrays. Classes allow data to be hidden from general access, and, typically, an iterator needs to be either a member function or a friend function of the class. The following example shows an iterator class associated with a safe vector class that provides ordered access to all elements:

```
//iterators : vector class

class  vector {
   friend class vector_iterator;
   int* v;
   int  sz;
public:
   vector(int);
   ~vector() { delete v; }

   int  size()  { return (sz); }
   int& operator[](int) ;
};

class  vector_iterator {
   int      cur_ind;
   vector* bv;
public:
   vector_iterator(vector& v) { bv = &v; cur_ind = 0; }
   int& next();
};
```

The iterator class `vector_iterator` has two private data members, both typical of such classes. The variable `cur_ind` is used to keep track of the ordering of element presentation. It is an index. The pointer variable `bv` is the reference to the associated vector variable. The constructor initializes these hidden variables. The member function next accesses each element in turn using cur_ind as its internal protected index into a variable of class vector.

The member function next is written as follows:

```
int& vector_iterator::next()
{
    if (cur_ind < bv -> sz)
        return (bv -> v[cur_ind++]);
    else {
        cur_ind = 0;
        return (bv -> v[cur_ind++]);
    }
}
```

This member function accesses private members of class vector and must be a friend of that class. The pointer variable bv is bound to an instance of class vector. The index variable cur_ind is autoincremented each time next is called, and is tested to make certain it does not exceed the internal vector element bound sz. It wraps around to 0 whenever it gets to this limit.

The following example shows how to use the iterator class to output the individual elements of a vector and contrasts this scheme with a traditional iteration:

```
ostream& operator<<(ostream& s, vector& w)
{
    s << "\nVECTOR  0 to " << w.size() - 1 << "\n";
    for(int i = 0; i < w.size(); ++i)
        s << dec(w[i], 8);
    s << "\n";
    return (s);
}
```

This is a standard style for overloading the stream operator << to output a variable of type vector. A traditional for loop is used to access elements of vector using public member functions. Now we will write a main function to output two vector variables:

```
main()
{
   vector            u(25), w(10);
   vector_iterator  w_it(w);

   for( int i = 0; i < u.size(); ++i)
       u[i] = i;
   cout << u;

   for( i = 0; i < w.size(); ++i)
       cout << (w_it.next() = 2 * i) << "\t";
}
```

The first for loop is traditional C. It initializes the vector u. The second for loop uses the iterator function next to initialize and print out consecutive values of the associated vector w.

8.6. An Example: Word Frequency

In this section we develop a multifile program using header files. The program will count the frequency of occurrence of words in a specified file, and will output an alphabetized list with each word's frequency.

Part of our purpose is to show how C++ lets you write programs quickly and modularly. We will reuse previously developed code. The binary search tree, which was discussed in Chapter 6, is a convenient and efficient means of storing this information.

```
//file bstree.h  binary search tree

typedef void (*pfct)(void*);
typedef void*  p_gen;

class bnode {
   friend class bstree;
   bnode* left;
   bnode* right;
   p_gen  data;
   int    count;
   bnode(p_gen d, bnode* l, bnode* r)
        { data = d; left = l; right = r; count = 1; }
   friend int comp(p_gen a, p_gen b);
   friend void prt(bnode* n);
};
```

```
class bstree {
    bnode* root;
public:
    bstree() { root = 0; }
    void   insert(p_gen d);
    p_gen find(p_gen d) { return (find(root, d)); }
    p_gen find(bnode* r, p_gen d);
    void   apply(pfct f) { traverse(root, f); }
    void   traverse(bnode* r, pfct f);
};
```

The class bstree is capable of storing a generic pointer and a count at each node of a binary search tree. It is a prototype class from which other classes are derived as needed.

```
//file stree.h

void prt(bnode* n);

int comp(p_gen i, p_gen j);

class s_tree : bstree {

public:
    s_tree() {}
    void   insert(char* d) { bstree::insert(p_gen(d)); }
    char* find(char* d)
        { return ((char* )bstree::find(p_gen(d))); }
    void print() { bstree::apply((pfct)prt); }
};
```

The class s_tree uses the insert function to store a pointer to char. In effect, each node will store a string. Each new word will be inserted as a string into the s_tree. The code for implementing these classes is stored in corresponding *.c files in order to allow separate compilation.

```
//file bstree.c
#include "bstree.h"

void bstree::insert(p_gen d)
{
    bnode* temp = root;
    bnode* old;

    if (root == 0) {
        root = new bnode(d, 0, 0);
        return;
    }
    while (temp != 0) {
        old = temp;
        if (comp(temp -> data, d) == 0) {
            (temp -> count)++;
            return;
        }
        if (comp(temp -> data, d) > 0)
            temp = temp -> left;
        else
            temp = temp -> right;
    }
    if (comp(old -> data, d) > 0)
        old -> left = new bnode(d, 0, 0);
    else
        old -> right = new bnode(d, 0, 0);
}

p_gen bstree::find(bnode* r, p_gen d)
{
    if (r == 0)
        return (0);
    else if (comp(r -> data, d) == comp(d, r -> data))
        return (r -> data);
    else if (comp(r -> data, d))
        return (find( r -> left, d));
    else
        return (find( r -> right, d));
}

void bstree::traverse(bnode* r, pfct f)
{
    if (r != 0) {
        traverse (r -> left, f);
        (*f)(r);
        traverse (r -> right, f);
    }
}
```

We have already discussed this code in Chapter 6.

```
//stree.c

#include "bstree.h"
#include "stree.h"
#include <string.h>
#include <stream.h>

void prt(bnode* n)
{
    cout << (char*)n -> data << "\t" ;
    cout << n -> count << "\t";
}

int comp(p_gen i, p_gen j)
{
    return (strcmp((char*)i, (char*)j));
}
```

The various *.h* files are necessary to provide appropriate definitions for these two functions. For example, strcmp is defined in *string.h* and cout is defined in *stream.h*. The prt function prints out a word and its frequency of occurrence as stored in count. The comp function lexicographically compares two strings. It is used for insertion into the binary search tree.

The next header file describes the function and constants related to extracting individual words from an istream:

```
//get_word.h

#include <ctype.h>
#include <stream.h>
enum boolean {false, true};
const maxlen = 80;
boolean get_word(char*, istream&);
```

Its corresponding *.c file is:

```
#include "get_word.h"

boolean  get_word(char* word_buf, istream& in)
{
   char  c;
   int   len = 0;

   while(in.get(c), !isalpha(c) && in.good())
      ;
   if (!in.good())
      return (false);
   else {
      word_buf[len++] = (isupper(c) ? tolower(c) : c);
      while (in.get(c), isalpha(c) && in.good())
         if (len < maxlen)
            word_buf[len++] = (isupper(c) ? tolower(c) : c);
      word_buf[len] = '\0';
      return (true);
   }
}
```

■ DISSECTION OF THE *get_word* FUNCTION

```
#include "get_word.h"
```

- This is the header file needed by this code. By separately compiling this code into an object file, for example, *get_word.o*, this routine can be conveniently used by any file that includes its header.

```
boolean  get_word(char* word_buf, istream& in)
```

- The input will be taken from an `istream`. The output will be a single word. If input fails then `false` is returned; if a word is found, then `true` is returned.

```
while(in.get(c), !isalpha(c) && in.good())
    ;
```

- The loop continues until an alphabetic character is detected. We use a comma expression. First a character is read into c; then it is tested. The loop also detects an end-of-file or an input failure.

```
if (!in.good())
    return (false);
```

- This indicates an input failure, normally an end-of-file.

```
word_buf[len++] = (isupper(c) ? tolower(c) : c);
while (in.get(c), isalpha(c) && in.good())
    if (len < maxlen)
        word_buf[len++] = (isupper(c) ? tolower(c) : c);
word_buf[len] = '\0';
return (true);
```

- This is the loop that collects the alphabetic characters into `word_buf`. A conversion to lowercase is made on all letters.

What remains is to put this all together into `main`.

```
//main for producing word frequencies
//Usage: executable  f1
//f1 must be present and readable
//An alphabetized word list is read to cout
//with frequency counts of all words in f1.

#include "bstree.h"
#include "stree.h"
#include "get_word.h"
#include <string.h>

main(int argc, char** argv)
{
   filebuf   f_in;

   if (argc != 2) {
      cout << "\nUsage:" << argv[0] << "  infile\n";
      exit(1);
   }
   if (!f_in.open(argv[1], input)) {
      cerr << "cannot open " << argv[1];
      exit(1);
   }

   istream   in(&f_in);
   s_tree    t;
   char      dat[80];
   char*     p;

   while (get_word(dat, in)) {
      p = new char[strlen(dat) + 1];
      strcpy(p, dat);
      t.insert(p);
   }
   t.print();
   cout << "\n\n\n";
}
```

The `main` function opens the input file for reading. It gets each word and stores it temporarily into `dat`. It stores the word permanently in a string created by `new`. This string is inserted into the search tree `t`. Finally, `t.print()` outputs the alphabetized word frequencies. Each piece of the code can be compiled separately.

8.7. OOP: Object-Oriented Programming

The central feature of OOP is its encapsulation of an appropriate set of data types and their operations. The class, with its member functions and operator overloading, provides an appropriate coding tool. Classes allow for the implementation of abstract data types.

A second feature is its promotion of code reuse through the inheritance mechanism. Without this reuse mechanism, each minor variation of an ADT would require code replication. Inheritance gives the programmer the ability to build a type hierarchy suitable to a particular problem domain.

A third feature is dynamic binding of types. The virtual function provides the ability to bind type at run-time. Thus an object determines how it is acted on. For example, let shape be a base class and draw and area be virtual functions in shape. Assume that there is a set of derived classes, such as rectangle, circle, pentagon, and triangle, and that each can know how to draw itself or compute its own area. A pointer to type shape can be used to dynamically process objects of any of the shape subtypes. Code for drawing shapes is more easily maintained because it is highly modular. New shape types can readily be added to with inheritance.

A fourth feature is data hiding. Access privileges can be managed and limited to whatever group of functions truly needs access to implementation details. The visibility modifiers public, protected, and private control client access to objects. This control promotes modularity and robustness.

The OOP programming task can be more difficult than normal procedural programming as found in C or Pascal. There is, for example, at least one extra design step before one gets to the coding of algorithms. This extra step involves the hierarchy of types that is useful for the problem at hand. Frequently one solves a problem more generally than is strictly necessary.

The extra step pays dividends in several ways. The solution is more encapsulated, which makes it more robust and easier to maintain and change, and also more reusable. For example, where the code needs a stack, that stack is easily borrowed from existing code. In an ordinary procedural language such a data structure is frequently "wired into" the algorithm and cannot be exported. All of these benefits are especially important for large coding projects that require coordination among many programmers. Here the ability to specify general interfaces for different classes allows each programmer to work on individual code segments with a high degree of integrity.

8.8. Summary

1. Multiple inheritance allows a derived class to inherit from more than one base class. The syntax of class headers is extended to allow a list, after the colon, of base classes and their privacy designation.

2. The early releases of C++ left unspecified the order of execution for initializing constructors in base and member constructors. With the addition of multiple inheritance, however, it became unnecessarily hazardous to continue this laxness. The current ordering is

   Explicit reference to base class constructors in the order in which they are listed after the header colon

   Unmentioned base classes in the order in which they are declared

   Explicit reference to member class constructors in the order in which they are listed after the header colon

3. For early C++ compilers, user types had, by default, bitwise assignment. Current systems default to a more sophisticated member-by-member assignment. This rule is recursive until components that are built-in types are assigned in the usual way. The same idea applies to default initialization.

4. A further change allows the operators `new` and `delete` to be overloaded. This feature provides a simple mechanism for user-defined manipulation of free store. Other technical changes include the ability to overload the operator `->`, distinguishing between signed and unsigned by the overloading selection algorithm, and the use of the scope resolution operator to define pointer to member types.

5. The standard system header file *stream.h* describes available stream I/O declarations, operations, and functions. However, the C++ system frequently provides other useful libraries accessible by including their corresponding *.h* files. Among these files are *complex.h, vec-*

tor.h, nlist.h, and *assert.h.* Many of these files describe system-provided classes. An example is *complex.h,* which provides a complex number data type.

6. Large C programs are partitioned into multifile units that can be compiled separately. Linking such separate modules requires resolving external references. In C++ these rules are explicit. The key rule is that external nonstatic variables must be defined in exactly one place. Static external constructs are local to a given file. Use of the keyword extern together with an initializer constitutes defining a variable. Using the keyword extern without an initializer constitutes a declaration but not a definition.

7. An iterator is a mechanism for accessing all components of a given type. The for statement provides a built-in iterator for simple arrays. Classes allow data to be hidden from general access, and, typically, an iterator needs to be either a member function or a friend function of the class.

8. C++ supports object-oriented programming (OOP). The central feature of this method is its encapsulation of an appropriate set of data types and their operations (ADTs). The class, with its member functions and operator overloading, provides an appropriate coding tool. A further key idea in OOP is its promotion of code reuse through the inheritance mechanism. The virtual function also provides the ability to bind type at run-time. Classes also provide data hiding. Access privileges can be managed and limited to whatever group of functions truly needs access to implementation details.

8.9. Exercises

1. What happens if you attempt to compile

```
struct A : B {
    int i;
};

struct B : A {
    int j;
};
```

2. From Section 8.1, use the `class plans` and the function `foo` to see how your compiler detects the inherent ambiguous reference to `cost`. Change the example to avoid this problem.

3. We want to write a portable factorial program. As written, the following program overflows on most machines:

```
#include <stream.h>
#include <limits.h>
#include <assert.h>

long fact(int n)
{
    if (n <= 1)
        return (1);
    else
        return (fact(n - 1) * n);
}

main()
{
    for (int i = 0; i < 25; ++i)
        cout << i << "  fact   " << fact(i) << "\n";
}
```

Add assertions to protect against system-dependent integer overflow.

4. The *assert.h* has the lines:

```
#ifdef NDEBUG
#define assert(EX)
     . . .
```

Explain how this allows a compiler flag to turn off the assertion mechanism.

5. If your system has a graphics library, see if you can draw a square on your screen.

6. From Section 8.5 we change the second `for` statement in `main` to the following:

```
for ( i = 0; i < w.size(); i += 2)
    cout << (w_it.next() = 2 * i) << "\t";
```

Explain what gets printed.

7. What if the `for` loop in the previous exercise were changed to the following:

```
for (i = 0; i < w.size(); ++i) {
   w_it.next() = 2 * i;
   cout << w_it.next() << "\t";
}
cout << w;
```

Explain what gets printed.

ASCII Character Codes

Left/Right Digits	ASCII American Standard Code for Information Interchange									
	0	**1**	**2**	**3**	**4**	**5**	**6**	**7**	**8**	**9**
0	nul	soh	stx	etx	eot	enq	ack	bel	bs	ht
1	nl	vt	np	cr	so	si	dle	dc1	dc2	dc3
2	dc4	nak	syn	etb	can	em	sub	esc	fs	gs
3	rs	us	sp	!	"	#	$	%	&	'
4	(	)	*	+	,	−	.	/	0	1
5	2	3	4	5	6	7	8	9	:	;
6	<	=	>	?	@	A	B	C	D	E
7	F	G	H	I	J	K	L	M	N	O
8	P	Q	R	S	T	U	V	W	X	Y
9	Z	[	\	]	^	_	`	a	b	c
10	d	e	f	g	h	i	j	k	l	m
11	n	o	p	q	r	s	t	u	v	w
12	x	y	z	{			}	~	del		

Some Observations

1. Character codes 0–31 and 127 are nonprinting.
2. Character code 32 prints a single space.
3. Character codes for digits 0 through 9 are contiguous.
4. Character codes for letters A through Z are contiguous.
5. Character codes for letters a through z are contiguous.

6. The difference between a capital letter and the corresponding
   lowercase letter is 32.

The Meaning of Some of the Abbreviations

nul	null	bel	bell	bs	backspace
ht	horizontal tab	nl	newline	vt	vertical tab
cr	carriage return	esc	escape		

APPENDIX B

Operator Precedence and Associativity

The following is the precedence and associativity table for all the C++ operators.

Operators	Associativity
::	left to right
() [] -> .	left to right
++ -- ! ~ sizeof (*type*) + (unary) - (unary) * (indirection) & (address) new delete delete[]	right to left
* / %	left to right
+ -	left to right
<< >>	left to right
< <= > >=	left to right
== !=	left to right
&	left to right
^ ~	left to right
|	left to right
&&	left to right
||	left to right
?:	right to left
= += -= *= /= *etc*	right to left
(comma operator)	left to right

In case of doubt, parenthesize.

APPENDIX C

C++ Additions To and Changes From C

This section is a brief summary of additions and changes to C++ from C. It is intended as a useful guide to the language.

1. KEYWORDS

Keywords are explicitly reserved identifiers that have a strict meaning in C++. They cannot be redefined or used in other contexts.

Keywords

auto	default	float	long	register	this
break	delete	for	new	return	typedef
case	do	friend	operator	short	union
char	double	goto	overload	sizeof	unsigned
class	else	if	private	static	virtual
const	enum	inline	protected	struct	void
continue	extern	int	public	switch	while

C++ implementations can have the additional keywords

```
asm catch signed template try volatile
```

Keywords not found in ANSI C are

class	delete	friend	inline	new	operator
overload	private	protected	public	this	virtual

2. CONSTANTS

Enumerations (Section 2.3) define named `int` constants. They can be anonymous, as in:

```
enum {false, true};
```

The keyword `const` (Section 2.2) is used to declare that an object's value is constant throughout its scope.

```
const int N = 100;
double w[N];            //Usually not allowed in ANSI C compilers
```

3. COMMENTS

C++ has a one-line comment symbol `//` (Section 2.1).

```
//Compile with version 1.2 or later
const float pi = 3.14159;  //pi accurate to six places
```

4. SCOPE RULES

Declarations can occur anywhere in a block (Sections 1.2, 2.3).

```
for (int i = 0; i < N; ++i) {
   . . .
```

Class member identifiers are local to that class. The scope resolution operator `::` can be used to resolve ambiguities (Section 2.5). Declarations cannot occur as initializing statements within nested loops. Selection statements such as the `if` or `switch` statement cannot only control a declaration. In general jumps and selections cannot bypass an initialization. This is not true in ANSI C.

```
class A {
public:
    int  i;
    void foo();
};

class B {
public:
    char i;
    void foo() {  A :: foo(); . . .}
};
```

A hidden external name can be accessed using the scope resolution operator.

```
int  i;
void  foo(int  i)
{
    i = ::i;
    . . .
}
```

A hidden class, struct, union, or enum identifier can be accessed by using its respective keyword.

```
static union u {
    . . .
};
void foo(int u)
{
    union u U;
    . . .
}
```

5. LINKAGE RULES

Linking separate modules requires resolving external references. The key rule is that external nonstatic variables must be defined in exactly one place (Section 8.4). Use of the keyword extern together with an initializer constitutes defining a variable. Using the keyword extern without an initializer constitutes a declaration but not a definition. The following example illustrates these rules.

```
//file prog1.c
  char  c;              //definition of c
  . . .


//file prog2.c
  extern char c;        //declaration of c
  . . .


//file prog3.c
  extern int n = 5;  //definition of n
  . . .


//file prog4.c
  char          c;     //illegal second definition
  extern float n;      //illegal type mismatch
  extern int    k;     //illegal no declaration
  . . .
```

Constant definitions and `inline` definitions can be duplicated. In general, it is good style to avoid the normal C program's reliance on the `#define` mechanism to produce simple constants and macros. One can also duplicate type definitions, function declarations, and enumerations.

6. TYPES

The fundamental types are as in C, with the following ANSI C extensions (Sections 2.3, 2.4, 2.6). Both `signed` and `void` types are available.

The derived types have significant extensions. These include generic pointer type `void*`. Both anonymous unions and anonymous enumerations are allowed, and there is also a reference type. The `class` type (Chapter 3) is another extension, and the `struct` is extended to be a variant of the `class`. Union, enumeration, and class names are type names.

```
void*    gen_ptr;                    //a generic pointer
int      i, &ref_i = i;              //ref_i is an alias for i
enum              {false, true};     //anonymous enumeration
enum boolean      {false, true};     //boolean is now a type name

class    card {                      //user-defined type
   int   cd;                         //private data member
public:
   suit s;                           //public data member
   pips p;
   void pr_card();                   //member function
};
```

7. CONVERSION RULES

Implicit pointer conversions occur in C++ (Section 5.1). Any pointer type can be converted to a generic pointer of type void*. The name of an array is a pointer to its base element. The null pointer value can be converted to any type. A pointer to a class can be converted to a pointer to a publicly derived base class (Section 6.4). This also applies to references. C++ is generally stricter than traditional C and does not allow mixing of pointer types unless they are correctly cast. As in ANSI C, float expressions need not be automatically converted to double.

Traditional C casts are augmented in C++ by a functional notation as a syntactic alternative (Section 5.2). A functional notation of the form

type-name (*expression*)

is equivalent to a cast. The type must be expressible as an identifier. Thus, the two expressions

```
x = float(i);    //C++ functional notation
x = (float) i;   //C   cast notation
```

are equivalent. Functional notation is the preferred style.

A constructor of one argument is de facto a type conversion from the argument's type to the constructor's class type. Consider an example of a `class string` constructor (Section 4.2):

```
string::string(char* p)
{
    len = strlen(p);
    s = new char[len + 1];
    strcpy(s, p);
}
```

This is automatically a type transfer from `char*` to `string`. These conversions are from an already defined type to a user-defined type. However, it is not possible for the user to add a constructor to a built-in type, for example, to `int` or `double`. In the string example, one may also want a conversion from `string` to `char*`. This can be done by defining a special conversion function inside the `string` class as follows:

```
operator (char *)() { return s; }    //recall char *s; is a member
```

The general form of such a member function is

```
operator type() { . . . }
```

These conversions occur implicitly in assignment expressions and in argument and return conversions from functions.

8. EXPRESSIONS AND OPERATORS

C++ introduces the operator `::` called the scope resolution operator. When used in the form `:: variable`, it allows access to the externally named variable (Section 2.5). Other uses of this notation are important for classes.

The unary operators `new` and `delete` are available to manipulate *free store* (Section 2.10). Free store is a system-provided memory pool for objects whose lifetime is directly managed by the programmer. The programmer creates the object by using `new` and destroys the object by using `delete`.

The operator `new` is used in the following forms:

```
new type-name
new type-name initializer
new (type-name)
```

In each case there are minimally two effects. First, an appropriate amount of store is allocated from free store to contain the named type. Second, the base address of the object is returned as the value of the `new` expression. The expression is of type `void*` and can be assigned to any pointer type variable. The operator `delete` destroys an object created by `new`, in effect returning its allocated storage to free store for reuse. The following example uses these constructs to dynamically allocate an array.

```
//Use of new operator to dynamically allocate an array.

#include <stream.h>

main()
{
    int* data;
    int  size;

    cout << "\nEnter array size: ";
    cin >> size;

    data = new int[size];
    for (int j = 0; j < size; ++j)
        cout << (data[j] = j) << "\t";
    cout << "\n\n";
    delete data;
    . . .
}
```

The pointer variable `data` is used as the base address of a dynamically allocated array whose number of elements is the value of `size`. The `new` operator is used to allocate from free store storage capable of storing an object of type `int[size]`. The operator `delete` returns to free store the storage associated with the pointer variable `data`. This can only be done with objects allocated by `new`. There are no guarantees on what values will appear in objects allocated from free store. The programmer is responsible for properly initializing such objects.

The operator `delete` is used in the following forms:

```
delete expression
delete [ expression ] expression
```

The first form is the most common. The expression is typically a pointer variable used in a previous `new` expression. The second form is occasionally used when returning store that was allocated as an array type. The bracketed expression gives the number of elements of the array. The operator `delete` returns a value of type `void`.

Almost all unary and binary operators may be overloaded. Precedence and associativity are as built-in.

9. CLASSES

The most significant addition to the language is the `class` (Chapter 3), which creates a user-defined type. An example is:

```
class vect {
    int* p;                              //base pointer
    int size;                            //numberer of elements
public:
    //constructors and destructor
    vect() { size = 10; p = new int[10]} //create a size 10 array
    vect(int n);                         //create a size n array
    vect(vect& v);                       //initialization by vect
    vect(int a[], int n);                //initialization by array
    ~vect() { delete p; }                //destructor
    //other member functions
    int  ub() { return (size - 1); } //upper bound
    int& operator [](int i);         //obtain range checked element
};
```

The keywords `public`, `private`, and `protected` indicate the visibility of members that follow (Sections 3.5, 6.2). The default for `class` is `private` and for `struct` is `public`. In the above example, the data members `p` and `size` are `private`. This makes them visible solely to member functions of the same class.

9.1. Constructors and Destructors

A constructor is a member function whose name is the same as the class name (Section 4.1). It *constructs* objects of the class type. This involves initialization of data members and frequently free store allocation using new. A destructor is a member function whose name is the class name preceded by the character ~ (Section 4.2). Its usual purpose is to *destroy* values of the class type. This is typically accomplished by using delete. A variable of a class having a destructor cannot be a member of a union.

For classes with constructors, if they have a constructor with a void argument list, then they can be a base type of an array declaration. Not all classes can have constructors, however. A variable of a class having a constructor cannot be a member of a union.

A constructor of the form

type: : *type* (*type*& x)

is used to perform copying of one *type* value into another when:

A *type* variable is initialized by a *type* value.

A *type* value is passed as an argument in a function.

A *type* value is returned from a function.

In older C++ systems, if this constructor is not present, then these operations were bitwise copy. In newer systems, the default is member-by-member assignment of value.

Classes with constructors having an empty argument list can have a derived array type. For example

```
vect a[5];
```

is a declaration that uses the empty argument constructor to create an array a of five objects, each of which is a size 10 vect.

A class having members whose type requires a constructor may have these specified after the argument list for its own constructor (Section 4.5). The constructor has a comma-separated list, following a colon, of constructor calls. The constructor is invoked by using the member name followed by a parenthesized argument list. In early versions of the C++ language the order of constructor invocation was unspecified. In

newer versions the order is as written in the comma-separated list, followed by any default initializations.

The keyword this denotes an implicitly declared self-referential
pointer (Section 4.8). It can be used in any non-static member function.
An obsolete use of this involved writing constructors and destructors
that use programmer-designed free store management functions.

9.2. Member Functions

Member functions are functions declared within a class and, as a con-
sequence, have access to private, protected, and public members of
that class (Section 3.4). If defined inside the class, they are treated as
inline functions and are also treated when necessary as overloaded
functions. In the class vect the member function

```
    int  ub() { return (size - 1); }              //upper bound
```

is defined. In this example, the member function ub is inline and has
access to the private member size.

Member functions are invoked normally by use of the "." or ->
operators, as in

```
    vect   a(20),  b;              //invoke appropriate constructor
    vect* ptr_v = &b;
    int    uba = a.ub(),  ubb;     //invoke member ub
    ubb = ptr_v -> ub();           //invoke member ub
```

9.3. Inheritance

Inheritance is the mechanism of *deriving* a new class from an old one
(Chapter 6). The existing class can be added to or altered to create the

derived class. A class can be derived from an existing class using the form:

> class *class-name* : (public|private) *optional* *base-class-name*
> {
>   *member declarations*
> };

As usual, the keyword class can be replaced by the keyword struct, with the usual implication that members are default public. The keywords public, private, and protected are available as visibility modifiers for class members (Section 6.2). A public member is visible throughout its scope. A private member is visible to other member functions within its own class. A protected member is visible to other member functions within its class and any class immediately derived from it. These visibility modifiers can be used within a class declaration in any order and with any frequency.

A base class having a constructor with arguments requires that a class derived from it have a constructor. The form of such a constructor is

> *class-name* (*argument list*) : (*base-class-name*) :
> (*base-class argument list*)
> {
>   . . .
> };

The base class argument list is used when invoking the appropriate base class constructor and is executed before the body of the derived class constructor is executed.

A publicly derived class is a *subtype* of its base class (Section 6.4). A variable of the derived class can in many ways be treated as if it were the base class type. A pointer whose type is pointer to base class can point to objects having the publicly derived class type. A reference to the derived class, when meaningful, may be implicitly converted to a reference to the public base class. It is possible to declare a reference to a base class and initialize it to an object of the publicly derived class.

The following is an example of a derived class:

```
class vect_bnd : public vect {
    int l_bnd, u_bnd;
public:
    vect_bnd();
    vect_bnd(int, int);
    int& operator[](int);
    int  ub() { return (u_bnd); }
    int  lb() { return (l_bnd); }
};

vect_bnd::vect_bnd() : vect(10)
{
    l_bnd = 0;
    u_bnd = 9;
}

vect_bnd::vect_bnd(int lb, int ub) : vect(ub - lb + 1)
{
    l_bnd = lb;
    u_bnd = ub;
}
```

In this example the constructors for the derived class invoke a constructor
in the base class with argument list following the colon.

What has been described is single inheritance. Current compilers
implement multiple inheritance (Section 8.1).

10. FUNCTIONS

Changes to how functions work include use of function prototypes, overloading, call-by-reference, default arguments, and the effects of the keywords inline, friend, and virtual.

10.1. Prototypes

In C++ the prototype form is (Section 2.5)

type name(argument-declaration-list);

Examples are:

```
double sqrt (double x);
void    pr_int (char*, int);        //definition contains names
void    ring_bell (void);           //function of no arguments
int     printf (char* format, ...); //variable number of args.
```

With the above sqrt prototype definition, invoking sqrt guarantees that, if feasible, an argument will be converted to type double. Prototypes are also found in ANSI C and greatly improve type checking.

10.2. Overloading

The term *overloading* refers to use of the same name for multiple meanings of an operator or a function (Section 2.9). The meaning selected will depend on the types of the arguments used by the operator or function (Section 5.3). C++ introduces the keyword overload to indicate that a particular name will be so used. This keyword is a function specifier. It is no longer necessary.

Consider a function that averages the values in an array of double versus one that averages the values in an array of int. Both are conveniently named avg_arr.

```
                                    //overload avg_arr;
                                    needed on early systems
double    avg_arr (double a[], int size);
double    avg_arr (int a[], int size);

double avg_arr (int a[], int size)
{
    int   sum = 0;

    for (int i = 0; i < size; ++i)
        sum += a[i];                //performs int arithmetic
    return ((double) sum / size);
}

double avg_arr (double a[], int size)
{
    double   sum = 0.0;

    for (int i = 0; i < size; ++i)
        sum += a[i];                //performs double arithmetic
    return (sum / size);
}
```

Overloaded functions are selected by matching the argument list of the function call to the argument list of the function declaration. A best match must be unique. It must be best on at least one argument and as good on all other arguments as any other match.

The matching algorithm for each argument is as follows:

Overloaded Function Selection Algorithm

1. Use an exact math if found.

2. Try standard type conversions.

3. Try user-defined conversions.

4. Use a match to ellipsis if found.

10.3. Call-by-Reference

Reference declarations allow C++ to have *call-by-reference* arguments (Section 2.7). Let us use this mechanism to write a function `greater` that exchanges two values if the first is greater than the second.

```
int greater(int& a, int& b)
{
   if (a > b) {              //exchange
      int temp = a;
      a = b;
      b = temp;
      return (1);
   }
   else
      return (0);
}
```

Now, if `i` and `j` are two `int` variables then

```
greater(i, j)
```

will use the reference to `i` and the reference to `j` to exchange, if necessary, their two values. In traditional C, this must be accomplished using pointers and indirection.

```
/* traditional C greater */
int greater(int* a, int* b)
{
    if (*a > *b) {               //exchange
        int temp = *a;
        *a = *b;
        *b = temp;
        return (1);
    }
    else
        return (0);
}
```

10.4. Inline

The keyword `inline` suggests to the compiler that the function be converted to inline code (Section 2.2). This keyword is used for the sake of efficiency and generally with short functions, and is implicit for member functions that are defined within their class. A compiler can ignore this directive for a variety of reasons, including the fact that the function is too long. In those cases, the `inline` function is compiled as an ordinary function. An example is:

```
inline float circum(float rad) { return (pi * 2 * rad); }
```

10.5. Default Arguments

A formal parameter can be given a default argument (Section 2.8). However, this can only be done with contiguous formal parameters that are right-most in the parameter list. A default value is usually an appropriate constant that occurs frequently when the function is called. The following function illustrates this point:

```
int mult(int n, int k = 2)              //k = 2 is default
{
    if (k == 2)
        return (n * n);
    else
        return (mult(n, k - 1) * n);
}
```

We assume that most of the time the function is used to return the value of n squared.

10.6. Friend Functions

The keyword `friend` is a function specifier (Section 5.4). It allows a nonmember function access to the hidden members of the class of which it is a friend. Its use is a method of escaping the strict strong typing and data hiding restrictions of C++. A `friend` function must appear inside the class declaration of which it is a friend. It is prefaced by the keyword `friend` and can appear anywhere in the class. Member functions of one class can be `friend` functions of another class. In this case the member function is written in the friend's class using the scope resolution operator to qualify its function name. If all member functions of one class are friend functions of a second class, this can be specified by writing `friend class` *class name*.

The following declarations are typical:

```
class tweedledee {
    . . .
    friend void alice();                //friend function
    int        cheshire();              //member function
    . . .
};

class tweedledum {
    . . .
    friend int tweedledee::cheshire();
    . . .
};

class tweedledumber {
    . . .
    friend class tweedledee;       //all member functions
                                   //of tweedledee have access
    . . .
};
```

10.7. Operator Overloading

A special case of function overloading is operator overloading (Section 5.5). The keyword `operator` is used to overload the built-in C operators. Just as a function name, such as `print`, can be given a variety of meanings that depend on its arguments, so can an operator, such as +, be given additional meanings. This allows infix expressions of both user types and built-in types to be written. The precedence and associativity remain fixed.

Operator overloading typically uses either member functions or friend functions because they both have privileged access. Overloading a unary operator using a member function has an empty argument list because the single operator argument is the implicit argument (Section 5.6). For binary operators, member function operator overloading has as the first argument the implicitly passed class variable and as a second argument the lone argument list parameter (Section 5.7). Friend functions or ordinary functions have both arguments specified in the parameter list.

We will demonstrate how to overload a unary operator using as an example ++. We define the class clock that can store time as days, hours, minutes, and seconds.

```
class clock {
    unsigned int  tot_secs, secs, mins, hours, days;
public:
    clock(unsigned int i);        //constructor and conversion
    void print();                 //formatted printout
    void tick();                  //add one second
    clock operator ++() { this -> tick(); return(*this); }
};
```

This class overloads the autoincrement operator. It is a member function and can be invoked on its implicit single argument. The member function tick adds one second to the implicit argument of the overloaded ++ operator.

10.8. Virtual Functions

The keyword virtual is a function specifier that provides a mechanism for dynamically selecting at run-time the appropriate member function from among base and derived class functions (Section 6.5). It may be used only to modify member function declarations. A virtual function must be executable code. When invoked, its semantics are the same as other functions. In a derived class, its name can be overloaded and the function prototype of the derived function must have matching type. The selection of which function to invoke from among a group of overloaded virtual functions is dynamic. The typical case is where a base class has a virtual function and derived classes have their versions of this function. A pointer to a base class type can point at either a base class object or a derived class object. The member function to be invoked is selected at run-time. It corresponds to the object's type not the pointer's type. In the absence of a derived type member, the base class virtual function is used by default.

Consider the following example:

```
//virtual function selection
#include <stream.h>

class B {
public:
    int   i;
    virtual void print_i () { cout << i << " inside B\n"; }
};

class D : public B {
public:
    void print_i () { cout << i << " inside D\n"; }
};

main ()
{
    B    b, *pb = &b;
    D    f;

    f.i = 1 + (b.i = 1);
    pb -> print_i ();
    pb = &f;
    pb -> print_i ();
}
```

The output from this program is

```
1 inside B
2 inside D
```

In each case a different version of print_i is executed. Selection depends dynamically on the object being pointed at.

11. STREAM I/O

C++ has been developing its own libraries distinct from C. The most important of these is described by *stream.h* (Chapter 7). This is the stream I/O library.

Output is returned to an object of type ostream. An operator << is overloaded in this class to perform output conversions from standard types. The standard output ostream corresponding to stdout is cout and the standard output ostream corresponding to stderr is cerr.

Formatted output (Section 7.2) is produced by using one of six standard functions: dec, oct, hex, chr, str, and form. These all return strings with the appropriate output representation. The function char* form(const char*, ...); has two nice properties that allow flexible use at a high level. First, a list of arguments of arbitrary length can be printed and, second, the printing is controlled by simple formats. The argument list to form has two parts:

control_string   and   *other_arguments*

It acts analogously to printf in C.

One can overload << to output user-defined types (Section 7.3). The operator << has two arguments, an ostream and the user type, and must produce an ostream. A typical function that does this is

```
ostream& operator<<(ostream& out, user type x)
{
    return(out << form(. . .));
}
```

Input is returned to an object of type istream as described in *stream.h* (Section 7.4). An operator >> is overloaded in this class to perform input conversions to standard types. The standard input istream corresponding to stdin is cin.

Each istream or ostream has an associated state that can be tested (Section 7.7). The states are as follows:

```
enum stream_state {_good, _eof, _fail, _bad};
```

This value is held in the private member variable state. The values for a particular stream can be tested using the overloaded public member function rdstate.

INDEX